SPOTLIGHT

D0380674

LIMA

ROSS WEHNER & RENÉE DEL GAUDIO

Contents

LIMA

LIMA

Lima's taxi drivers tend to be educated, perceptive, and opinionated. When asked what they think about Lima, they will tick off a litany of complaints: The highways are congested with buses. The air is full of exhaust and noise. Slums have sprawled across all the desert hills around Lima and residents there lack regular plumbing, water, and sometimes even electricity. The city's politicians and business leaders create a daily circus of corruption, and there is a huge, and growing, separation between the rich and the poor. Then, as if that weren't enough, there's the *garúa*. The blanket of fog rolls in from the ocean and covers everything May–November, depositing a patina of grime that lends the city its gray, dismal appearance.

But, in the same breath, the taxi driver will extol the virtues of this once-opulent capital of the Spanish viceroyalty that stretched from present-day Ecuador to Chile. Limeños are an exotic cocktail, a bit of coast, sierra, and jungle blended with African, Chinese, and European to create an eclectic, never-before-seen blend. Heaps of tangy ceviche and succulent shellfish can be had for a few dollars, along with shredded chicken served in a creamy concoction of milk, mountain cheese, nuts, and *ají* pepper. Bars, clubs, and local music venues, called *peñas,* explode most nights with dance and the rhythms of *cumbia,* salsa, Afro-Peruvian pop, and a dozen forms of creole music. There are sandy beaches just a half hour south of the city. And despite all its griminess, the center of Lima shines forth with a wealth of colonial art and architecture, rivaled perhaps only by

HIGHLIGHTS

Catedral: After two decades of turbulence, the center of Lima is roaring back, and at the center of It all is a refurbished main square and the 16th-century cathedral, with elegantly carved choir stalls and a huge painting gallery (page 12).

Casa de Aliaga: This colonial mansion in the heart of Lima's old town is in pristine condition and offers a fascinating glimpse into domestic life during the opulent days of the viceroyalty (page 16).

San Francisco: This 16th-century convent has a brightly decorated patio and

painting gallery upstairs, and labyrinthian catacombs downstairs that served for centuries as Lima's general cemetery (page 17).

Museo Larco: With a huge collection of gold, textiles, and more than 40,000 ceramics, this museum offers a complete survey of all of Peru's archaeological treasures (page 19).

Museo Nacional de Arqueología: The best way to wrap your mind around Peru's complex succession of ancient cultures is by visiting this compact and concise museum (page 20).

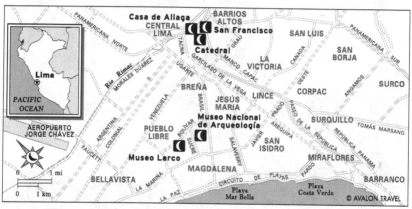

LOOK FOR **C** TO FIND RECOMMENDED SIGHTS, ACTIVITIES, DINING, AND LODGING.

Mexico City, the other great center of Spanish power in the New World.

The bottom line: Lima is an extraordinary city, but it takes a little getting used to. The country's leading museums, churches, and restaurants are here, along with nearly eight million people, almost a third of Peru's population. It is the maximum expression of Peru's cultural diversity (and chaos). Whether you like it or not, you will come to Lima, because nearly all international flights land at this gateway. But do yourself a favor and see Lima at the end of your trip, not at the beginning. That way you

have a better chance of understanding what you see and not becoming overwhelmed in the process.

PLANNING YOUR TIME

Depending on your interests, Lima can be seen in a day's dash or several days to take in most of the museums, churches, and surrounding sights. Peru travelers tend to enjoy Lima more at the end of a trip than at the beginning. After visiting Puno, Cusco, and other Peruvian cities, travelers are more prepared to deal with the logistics of getting around this huge city. They

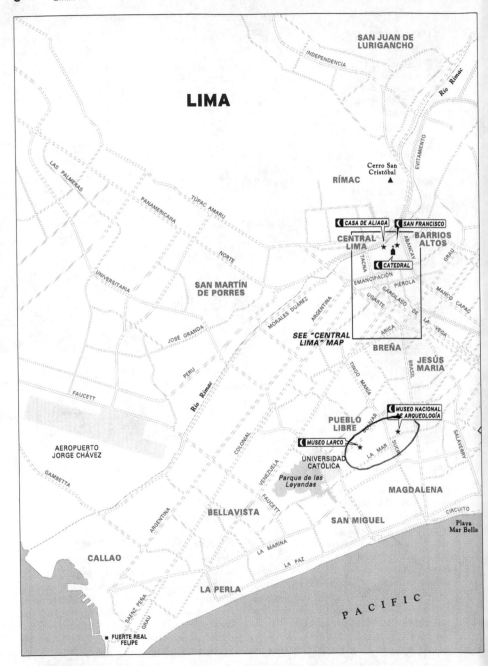

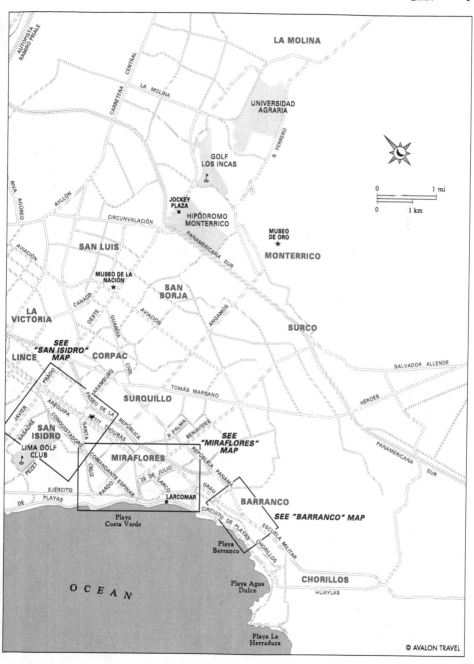

LA MOLINA

AUTOPISTA RAMIRO PRIALE

CARRETERA CENTRAL

LA MOLINA

UNIVERSIDAD
AGRARIA

R. FERRERO

GOLF
LOS INCAS

RIVA

AGÜERO

AYLLÓN

JOCKEY
PLAZA

CIRCUNVALACIÓN

HIPÓDROMO
MONTERRICO

PANAMERICANA SUR

MUSEO
DE ORO
★

AVIACIÓN

SAN LUIS

MONTERRICO

MUSEO DE LA
NACIÓN
★

SAN
BORJA

LA
VICTORIA

CANADÁ

OESTE

GUARDIA

AVIACIÓN

ANGAMOS

SURCO

SEE
"SAN ISIDRO"
MAP

LINCE

CORPAC

CIVIL

SALVADOR ALLENDE

PRADO

ARAMBURU

PASEO DE LA

TOMÁS MARSANO

SURQUILLO

HÉRDES

JAVIER

BASADRE

AREQUIPA

CONQUISTADORES

SANTA

PETIT THOUARS

REPÚBLICA

R PALMA

BENAVIDES

SEE
"MIRAFLORES"
MAP

SAN
ISIDRO

LIMA GOLF
CLUB

PEZET

COMANDANTE ESPINAR

CRUZ

MIRAFLORES

REPÚBLICA, PANAMA

PANAMERICANA

28 DE JULIO

LARCO

SUR

EJÉRCITO

PARDO ESPINAR

GRAU

DE

PLAYAS

LARCOMAR

CIRCUITO DE PLAYAS

BARRANCO

SEE "BARRANCO" MAP

Playa
Costa Verde

ESCUELA MILITAR

CHORILLOS

Playa
Barranco

OCEAN

Playa Agua
Dulce

CHORILLOS

HUAYLAS

Playa La
Herradura

© AVALON TRAVEL

0   1 mi

0   1 km

have also seen enough of the country to make better sense of the vast, and often poorly explained, collections in Peru's museums. Things start making sense.

If you are short on time and are visiting Cusco, one headache-free option is to fly from Cusco to Lima early in the morning and spend the day touring Lima on an organized tour (if you are planning on seeing Lima on your own, plan on one day for just acclimatizing). Various good day tours include lunch at one of the better restaurants in the city. In the evening, you can head to the airport for your flight home.

This is also a good way to avoid a long layover at Lima's unpleasant airport. Because of afternoon winds, most flights leave Cusco in the morning. But from Lima, international flights tend to leave in the evening. So travelers coming from Cusco often end up spending several hours at Lima's airport on their way home.

HISTORY

Present-day Lima was never the center of any great empire but rather a verdant valley where a series of cultures flourished alongside the shrine of **Pachacámac,** which by the Inca's time housed one of the most respected, and feared, oracles in the Andes. Huaca Pucllana, in Lima's upscale Miraflores neighborhood, was a ceremonial center built out of adobe bricks by the seafaring **Lima culture** from around A.D. 200 onward. The valley later fell under the influence of the Ayacucho-based **Huari culture** and was integrated by 1300 into the **Ychma kingdom,** which built most of the monumental architecture at Pachacámac. Inca **Túpac Yupanqui** conquered the area in the mid-15th century and built an enclosure for holy women alongside Pachacámac's stepped pyramid.

The first Spaniard to arrive in the area was **Hernando Pizarro,** who rode with a group of soldiers from Cajamarca in 1533 to investigate reports of gold at Pachacámac. They found nothing, but his brother, Francisco, returned two years later to move the capital here from Cusco. **Francisco Pizarro** was drawn to the spot because of its fertile plains and the natural

port of Callao. (Both Pizarros had come here in January, in the middle of Lima's brief summer, and must have thought it was a sunny place!)

Pizarro laid the city out in typical checkerboard pattern, with the main square butting up against the **Río Rímac** ("talking river" in Quechua), a natural defensive line. He christened Lima **Ciudad de Los Reyes** (City of the Kings), and a decade later it was designated the capital of the Spanish viceroyalty in South America and eventually seat of the continent's archbishop. **Universidad San Marcos,** America's first university, was founded here in 1511, and the city was completely walled by the 17th century.

Most of the Catholic orders established themselves in Lima and built more than a dozen baroque churches and convents. Even the Spanish Inquisition for South America was based here (its headquarters is now an interesting museum). By royal decree all the commerce of the entire viceroyalty—essentially the entire west side of South America—had to pass through Lima, fueling a construction boom of elegant homes and promenades, such as the Paseo de Aguas on the far side of the Río Rímac (these days a downtrodden neighborhood).

The city was quickly rebuilt after a devastating 1746 earthquake that destroyed 80 percent of the city and slammed the port of **Callao** with a 12-meter tsunami. Lima's prominence began to fade after the independence wars of the 1820s, when it lost its monopoly over South American commerce.

Even in the early days of Lima, neighborhoods of black, mulatto, Indian, and mestizo workers began to crop up around the city, and the expansion continued after the city's walls were torn down by **President José Balta** (1868–1872). During the **War of the Pacific** (1879–1883), Lima was sacked by an invading Chilean army, which carted off church gold and most of the national library's books to Santiago de Chile.

There had always been a main avenue leading through the countryside to the port of Callao, but as the city expanded, other principal avenues were built outside the center, and

© ANIBAL SOLIMANO, PROMPERU

Balconies are for Limeños what the Eiffel Tower is for the French – an unequivocal stamp of national character.

the city's first electric train was inaugurated in 1906. For four centuries Lima had been a small city and even in 1919 only had 173,000 inhabitants. Over the rest of the 20th century, Lima's population would swell 44-fold to its current population of nearly eight million.

As in La Paz, Bolivia, and other South American capitals, Lima's population exploded as the country transitioned from a rural economy to one based on large industry. Impoverished campesinos immigrated here from the countryside and built ramshackle slums, called *pueblos jóvenes*. Since the mid-1990s, these slums have turned into full-fledged neighborhoods, albeit poor neighborhoods. Regardless, they no longer lack water and sewer service and have Internet and big grocery stores.

Lima's poverty became intense during the 1980s and 1990s, when a series of countryside massacres committed by both the **Shining Path** and the Peruvian army sparked a crushing migration to Lima. The new immigrants worked at whatever they could find, and many ended up becoming street vendors

(*ambulantes*), causing the center's main streets to become completely congested. After being elected in 1990, **President Alberto Fujimori** put an end—albeit through corrupt techniques which now have him exiled in Chile—to the rampant inflation, rolling blackouts, and car bombings that were terrorizing Lima residents. In 1992, he captured Shining Path leader **Abimael Guzmán. Túpac Amaru,** the country's other main guerilla group, staged a final stand in Lima in 1996 by taking 490 hostages during a gala at the Japanese ambassador's residence. The standoff ended four months later after a Peruvian special forces team freed the hostages, killing the 14 guerillas in the process (only one hostage died—of bleeding from a gunshot wound).

Even before the terrorism years, much of the commerce and most of the wealthy families had abandoned the center of Lima and established the upscale neighborhoods and corporate centers of Monterrico, Miraflores, and San Isidro, where nearly all of the city's best hotels and restaurants are now located.

Though still a bit grimy and unsafe to walk around in at night, the center of Lima is making a comeback. Street vendors were banned in the mid-1990s, and now the Plaza de Armas has been renovated with new riverside promenades and a spate of nice restaurants. Businesses like *Caretas,* the country's leading newsmagazine, have moved back to the center. Compared to the mid-1990s, the center of Lima feels pleasant and safe.

Sights

Lima can be thought of as a triangle, with the center at the apex. The base begins with the port of **Callao** and the nearby airport and runs along the coast through the neighborhoods of **Miraflores, Barranco,** and **Chorillos.** Other neighborhoods, such as **Pueblo Libre** and **San Isidro,** are in the middle of the triangle.

Lima is jam-packed with sights, but most interesting to many people are the colonial churches, convents, and homes in Lima's center, which is safe but warrants precautions nonetheless: Leave your passport and money in the hotel, and guard your camera.

Lima's best museums are spread out, set in neighborhoods that are sandwiched between the coast and the center. Excellent collections of pre-Columbian gold, textiles, and ceramics can be found at the Museo Larco in Pueblo Libre, Museo de la Nación in San Borja, and Museo de Oro in Monterrico. English- and sometimes French-speaking guides are usually available at these museums.

Most Lima visitors stay in San Isidro, Miraflores, and Barranco, neighborhoods near the coast with the best selection of hotels, restaurants, and nightlife. There is little to see here, however, except for giant adobe platforms that were built by the Lima culture (A.D. 200–700) and now rise above the upscale neighborhoods.

There are so many sights to see in downtown Lima that you would need a few days to see them all. The best idea is to start early with the big sights, be selective, and work your way down the list as energy allows. The old town is bordered by the Río Rímac to the north, Avenida Tacna to the west, and Avenida Abancay to the east. The center of Lima is perfectly safe, but it is a good idea not to stray too far outside these main streets—except for a lunchtime foray to Chinatown or a taxi ride to Museo de los Descalzos, on the other side of the river. Mornings are best reserved for visits to Lima's main churches, which are mostly open 8 A.M.–1 P.M. and 5–8 P.M. daily and have English-speaking guides who request a tip only. Taxis into the center from Miraflores cost US$5 (15–30 minutes), or on Arequipa Avenue catch a Todo Arequipa bus that runs to within walking distance of the center (US$0.50, 20–50 minutes).

CENTRAL LIMA AND PUEBLO LIBRE
C Catedral

Start on the **Plaza Mayor,** which is graced with a bronze fountain from 1650 and flanked on one side by the Catedral, which was built in the late 16th century. It contains the carved wooden sepulcher of Francisco Pizarro, who was murdered in 1541 by a mob of Almagristas, a rival political faction. As you enter, the first chapel on the right is dedicated to St. John the Baptist and contains a carving of Jesus that is considered to be among the most beautiful in the Americas. But the highlights of the cathedral are the choir stalls carved in the early 17th century by Pedro Noguera and the museum (9 A.M.–4:30 P.M. Mon.–Fri., 10 A.M.–4:30 P.M. Sat., US$5). Paintings here include a 1724 work by Alonso de la Cueva that paints the faces of the 13 Inca rulers alongside a lineup of Spanish kings from Carlos V to Felipe V. There is no clearer example of how art was used to put order on a turbulent, violent succession of kings. Other pieces include a series of allegorical paintings painted in the 17th century by the Bassano brothers in northern Italy (no one knows how or when this priceless art was imported) and chest altars, one from Ayacucho and the other from Cusco, with an astounding number of miniature painted figures made of potato flour.

Also on the Plaza Mayor are the magnificent **Archbishop's Palace** (not open to the public) and, on the corner, the **Casa del Oidor.** This 16th-century house is closed to the public but has Lima's signature wooden balconies on the outside, with carvings inspired by Moorish designs and wood slats from behind which women viewed the activity on the square. Next door is the **Palacio del Gobierno,** the president's palace, which forms the other side of the Plaza Mayor and was built by the Spanish on top of the home of Taulichusco, the ruler of the Rímac Valley at that time. It was at this spot that liberator Jose de San Martín proclaimed the symbolic independence of Peru on July 28, 1821. There is an interesting change of the guard at noon and a change of the flag at 5:45 P.M. Monday–Saturday.

Also on the Plaza Mayor is the **Club de la Unión,** a business club formed in 1868 that is a bit empty these days, are also on the Plaza Mayor. Between these buildings are the pedestrian streets of Pasaje Santa Rosa and Escribanos, which are lined with upscale restaurants, cafés, and bookstores. At the corner of the palace and the Municipality is Lima's antique post office, the **Casa de Correos**

COLONIAL VS. REPUBLICAN HOMES

The differences between colonial (1534-1822) and republican homes (1820-1900) are clear in theory but muddled in practice. Most of Peru's old homes were built in colonial times by Spaniards who received the prized plots on or near the Plaza de Armas. These houses, passed down from generation to generation, were often restored in the 19th or early 20th century with republican elements. So most houses, or casonas, are somewhat of a blend.

But all share in common the basic Spanish layout: a tunnel-like entry, or zaguán, leads into a central courtyard, or traspatio. The rooms are built with high ceilings and a second-story wood balcony around the courtyard. Rich homes have stone columns, instead of wood, and additional patios.

During the nearly three centuries of the Peruvian viceroyalty, homes went from the solid, fortified, construction of medieval times to the more intricate decorations of the baroque, which were often based on Mudejar, or Arabic, patterns brought from Spain. After independence, however, homes demonstrate neoclassic elegance and a more confident use of colors favored in the New World, such as bright blues, greens, and yellows.

COLONIAL HOMES

- Traspatios paved with canto rodado (river stones)

- Sparse interiors

- Heavy brown and green colors

- Simple ceilings, often made of plaster, cane, and tile

- Baroque or rococo decorations with Mudejar patterns

- Forged iron windows with intricate lace patterns

- Celosia balconies where women could observe but not be observed

REPUBLICAN HOMES

- Traspatios paved with polished stone slabs

- Elegant interior decorations and furniture

- Light yellow, white, and blue colors

- Elaborate, often carved, wooden ceilings

- Neoclassic decorations with ornate columns

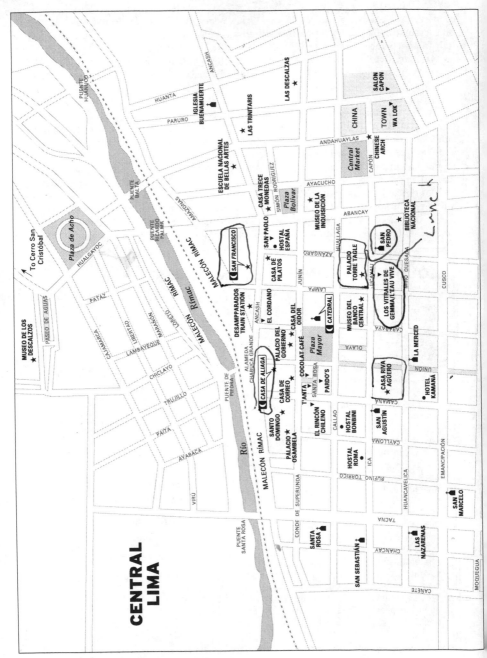

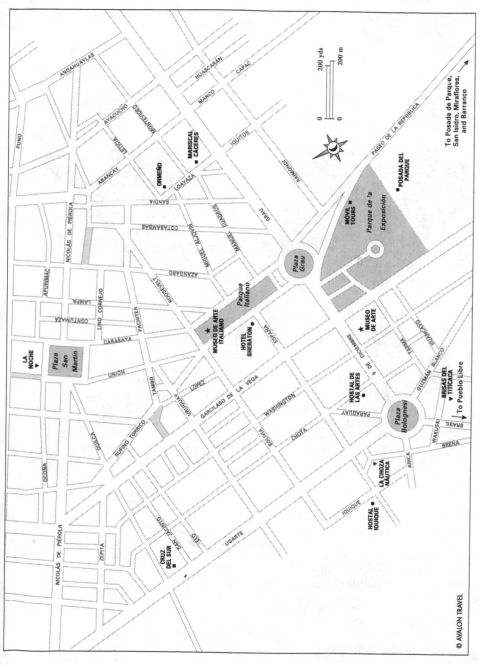

© AVALON TRAVEL

Lima's Catedral, built in the late 16th century, is a must-see.

y Telégrafos (176 Conde de Superunda, 8 A.M.–8 P.M. Mon.–Sat., 8 A.M.–4 P.M. Sun.), which has a small stamps museum. Behind the post office is the pedestrian walkway **Pasaje de Correos,** which had a glass roof until a 1940 earthquake and is now lined with vendors selling postcards, teddy bears, and other miscellaneous items.

◖ Casa de Aliaga

A half block from the Plaza Mayor down Unión is Casa de Aliaga (Unión 224), which was built in 1535 and is the oldest home on the continent still family owned after 17 generations. It is one of the best-preserved colonial homes in Peru, with a series of salons representing decor from the 16th, 17th, and 18th centuries. The land for the home was first deeded to Jerónimo de Aliaga, one of the 13 men who remained with Francisco Pizarro during his grueling exploration of Peru's coast in 1527. All visits must be arranged in advance through Lima Tours (tel. 01/619-6900).

Santo Domingo and Lima Riverfront

Near the Plaza Mayor is Santo Domingo,

which is on the corner of Camaná and Conde de Superunda. This church was built in 1537 by the Dominicans and was remodeled in neoclassic style in the 19th century. At the end of the right nave is the Retablo de las Reliquias (Altar of the Relics), with the skulls of the three Peruvian Dominicans to reach sainthood. From left to right, they are San Martín de Porras, Santa Rosa, and San Juan Macias. Next door is the attached convent (9 A.M.–12:30 P.M. and 3–6 P.M. Mon.–Sat., 9 A.M.–1 P.M. Sun., US$3), with carved balconies around a patio, fountains covered with Seville tiles, and a library with colossal 17th-century choir books. This convent was the first location of America's first university, **San Marcos,** and the balcony where students read their theses can still be seen in the Sala Capitular. Also on the street Conde de Superunda is **Palacio Osamblea** (Superunda 298, 9:30 A.M.–5 P.M. Mon.–Fri., free), a neoclassic, rose-colored home with five elegant balconies. It has been converted into a space for revolving exhibitions hosted by the Centro Cultural Garcilaso de la Vega.

Alameda Chabuca Grande is a new riverfront public space, within a block of the Plaza

the interior courtyard of Palacio Osamblea

Mayor, that is dedicated to one of Peru's best-known musicians, whose creole music is famous worldwide. This used to be the sprawling Polvos Azules market, which was shut down by the government in 2000 and moved to its present location along the Vía Expresa. The space is now used by musicians and artists and is generally safe to walk around until 9 P.M., when the security guards go home.

The Río Rímac, brown with mud and clogged with plastic, tumbles by here. Across the river, the Rímac neighborhood was populated by mestizos and mulattos during colonial times. The large hill on the other side is **Cerro San Cristóbal.** Walk upriver along Ancash to **Desamparados,** Lima's beautiful old station, which is being converted into a cultural center with revolving exhibits.

San Francisco

San Francisco (Ancash and Lampa, 9:15 A.M.–5:45 P.M. daily, US$3.50, US$1.75 students) is a 16th-century convent featuring a patio lined with centuries-old *azulejos* (Sevillean tiles) and

roofed with *machimbrado,* perfectly fitted puzzle pieces of Nicaraguan mahogany. There are frescoes from the life of Saint Francis of Assisi, a 1656 painting of the Last Supper with the disciples eating guinea pig and drinking from gold Inca cups (*qeros*), and a series of paintings from Peter Paul Rubens's workshop depicting the passion of Christ. But the highlight is the catacombs, or public cemetery, where slaves, servants, and others without money were buried until 1821 (rich citizens were usually buried in their home chapels). The underground labyrinth is a series of wells, some 20 meters deep, where bodies were stacked and covered with lime to reduce odor and disease. After they decomposed, the bones were stacked elsewhere. Across the street from San Francisco is Casa de Pilatos (Ancash 390, closed to the public), a colonial home that is occupied by Peru's Constitutional Tribunal.

Museo de la Inquisición

Casa de las Trece Monedas (Ancash 536, closed to the public) was built in 1787 and gets its name from the 13 coins in the coat of arms on its facade. Nearby is **Plaza Bolívar,** flanked by Peru's congress building and graced with a bronze statue in honor of liberator Simón Bolívar. On the far side of the plaza is the interesting **Museo de la Inquisición** (www.congreso.gob.pe/museo.htm, 9 A.M.–5 P.M. daily, free), which served as the headquarters of the Spanish Inquisition from 1570 until it was abolished in 1820. The museum explains the harsh and bizarre punishments that the church doled out for crimes ranging from heresy and blasphemy to seduction and reading banned books. There are creepy dungeonlike spaces in the back where the punished were given 50 lashes and jailed while others were sent to work on slave ships or in public hospitals. This was also where autos-da-fé were ordered—public condemnation ceremonies in the Plaza de Armas where witches, bigamists, and heretics were hung to death or burned at the stake.

Chinatown

Chinatown is an excellent place to have lunch

or late-afternoon tea, in the midst of a neighborhood founded by Chinese indentured workers, or coolies, who came here after finishing their contract on the train lines or coastal haciendas. The main street is **Capón,** which has three **Asian temples,** a **Chinese arch,** and a variety of stores and restaurants. The entire Chinatown area is adjacent to Lima's **central market.**

Historic Downtown

The 16th-century **San Pedro** (Azángaro and Ucayali, hours vary, free) has a drab mannerist facade but is one of the most spectacular church interiors in Peru. Huge white arching ceilings lead to a magnificent altar covered in gold leaf and designed by Matías Maestro, who is credited for bringing the neoclassic style to Peru. At the end of the right nave, ask permission to see the mind-blowing sacristy, decorated with tiles and graced with a magnificent painting of the coronation of the Virgin Mary by Peru's most famous painter, Bernardo Bitti. Painted on the ceiling boards above are scenes of the life from San Ignacio. If you come in the morning, it is possible to ask permission to see the cloisters and two interior chapels as well.

Palacio Torre Tagle

© RENEE DEL GAUDIO AND ROSS WEHNER

Palacio Torre Tagle (Ucayali 363) is a mansion built in 1735 that is, like Casa de Aliaga, in pristine condition. Visits can be arranged by popping into the Ministry of Foreign Affairs next door at Ucayali 318. At the **Museo del Banco Central** (tel. 01/613-2000, 10 A.M.–4:30 P.M. Tues. and Thurs.–Fri., 10 A.M.–7 P.M. Wed., free), the ground floor holds a colonial money exhibit, one flight up is a 19th- and 20th-century painting gallery, and the basement shines with pre-Columbian ceramics and textiles (including a range of intriguing Chanca pieces). The paintings include a good selection of watercolors from Pancho Fierro (1807–1879), paintings from 20th-century artist Enrique Polanco, and etchings by Cajamarca's indigenous artist José Sabogal (1888–1956).

The church of **San Agustín** (corner of Ica and Camaná, hours vary, free) has an 18th-century baroque facade that is one of the most intricate in the Americas and looks almost as if it were carved from wood, not stone. **Casa Riva Agüero** (Camaná 459, 10 A.M.–1 P.M. and 2–8 P.M. Mon.–Sat., US$7, US$1.75 museum only), an 18th-century home with all original furniture, has an interesting museum of colonial handicrafts as well as ceramics and textiles from the Lima culture.

Other interesting churches, which are clustered together, are **La Merced** (Unión and Miró Quesada, hours vary, free), which was built in 1754 and holds a baroque retablo carved by San Pedro de Nolasco, and **San Marcelo** (Rufino Torrico and Emancipación, hours vary, free). Nearby there is a string of three 17th-century churches within four blocks of each other on the busy Avenida Tacna: **Las Nazarenas** (6 A.M.–noon and 5–8:30 P.M. daily), which holds the image of El Señor de los Milagros, the city's patron saint whose October festival draws as many as a half million celebrants; **San Sebastián** (hours vary, free); and **Santa Rosa** (9:30 A.M.–noon and 3:30–7 P.M. daily).

Art Museums

If you are taking a taxi from San Isidro or Miraflores into the center, you will travel along a sunken highway known as the **Vía Expresa** (also nicknamed "El Zanjón," or The Ditch). The highway emerges on ground level and passes along a series of public parks before entering old town. One of these is the **Parque de la Exposición,** which was built in the 19th century and is still thriving today. The park is ringed with a high fence and is best entered at the corner of 28 de Julio and Inca Garcilaso de la Vega. Nearby is an artificial lake with paddleboats and the **Kusi Kusi Puppet Theatre** (basement of the German-style gingerbread house, tel. 01/477-4249), which has Sunday performances listed in the cultural section of the *El Comercio* newspaper. Here too is the **Museo de Arte** (Paseo Colón 125, Parque de la Exposición, tel. 01/423-4732, http://museoarte.perucultural.org.pe, 10 A.M.–5 P.M. Thurs.–Tues., US$5.50 adult, US$3.75 students), which houses the best range of Peruvian paintings in the country, an espresso bar, and a cinema. The museum contains colonial furniture, some pre-Columbian ceramics, and a huge collection of paintings from the viceroyalty to the present. Another nearby park is the **Parque Italiano,** which contains the **Museo de Arte Italiano** (Paseo de la República 250, tel. 01/423-9932, 10 A.M.–5 P.M. Mon.–Fri., US$3), with a collection of European art mainly from the early 20th century.

Rímac

Right across the Río Rímac from Lima is the downtrodden Rímac neighborhood, which began as a mestizo and mulatto barrio during the viceroyalty and was refurbished in the 18th century by the Lima aristocracy. All the sights here are close to the Plaza de Armas—take a taxi, as assaults are common in this area.

The **Museo de los Descalzos** (end of Alameda Los Descalzos, tel. 01/482-3360, 10 A.M.–1 P.M. and 3–6 P.M. Tues.–Sat., 11:30 A.M.–6 P.M. Sun.) was a convent and spiritual retreat for the Franciscans. Today it contains interesting and elegant cloisters,

a chapel with a gold-covered baroque altar, an elegant refectory, and a gallery with more than 300 paintings from the 17th and 18th century—including a masterpiece by Esteban de Murillo. On the taxi ride home, ask your taxi driver to pass the nearby **Paseo de Aguas,** an 18th-century French-style promenade where Lima's elites strolled along its artificial waterways. All that remains today is a neoclassic arch, hidden next to a towering Cristal Beer factory. Nearby is the giant **Plaza de Acho,** Lima's bullring, where **bullfights** are held early October–early December. Inside is the **Museo Taurino** (Hualgayoc 332, tel. 01/481-1467, 9 A.M.–6 P.M. Mon.–Sat., US$1.50), which contains a wide range of bullfighting relics.

Towering above Rímac is **Cerro San Cristóbal,** where Francisco Pizarro placed a cross in thanks that Quizo Yupanqui and his Inca army did not succeed in crossing the Río Rímac into Lima during the Inca rebellion of 1536. Today the hill is encrusted with a dusty *pueblo jóven* named Barrios Altos. There is a lookout over Lima at the top, along with a small museum and a giant cross that is illuminated at night. To reach the top, take a taxi from the Plaza de Armas (US$6) or wait for buses with English-speaking guides that leave from the Municipality (US$3.50).

◖ Museo Larco

The charming neighborhood of **Pueblo Libre** is just south of central Lima and has a relaxed, small-town vibe. Its best-known sight is the Museo Larco (Bolívar 1515, tel. 01/461-1312, www.museolarco.org, 9 A.M.–6 P.M. daily, US$11), which rivals the Museo de Oro in terms of gold pieces and has far more ceramics and textiles. Founded in 1926 in an 18th-century mansion built atop a pre-Hispanic ruin, this museum has more than 40,000 ceramics and 5,000 pieces of gold and textiles. There are huge Mochica earrings and funerary masks, a Paracas textile with a world-record 398 threads per inch, and a jewelry vault filled with gold and silver objects. A back storage room holds thousands of pre-Hispanic ceramic vessels, including a Moche erotic collection that will cause even the most liberated to blush. There is an excellent on-site restaurant, and it is easy to reach by bus from Miraflores. Catch a bus at Arequipa Avenue that says Todo Bolívar and get off at the 15th block.

◖ Museo Nacional de Arqueología

A 15-minute walk away from Museo Larco is Pueblo Libre's laid-back Plaza Bolívar and the Museo Nacional de Arqueología, Antropología, e Historia (Plaza Bolívar s/n, Pueblo Libre, tel. 01/463-5070, http://museonacional.perucultural.org.pe, 9:30 A.M.–5 P.M. Tues.–Sat., US$5 including tour). Though smaller than the Museo de la Nación, this museum presents a clearer, certainly more condensed, view of Peruvian history, and linked with the Museo Larco it makes for a complete day in central Lima. Exhibits include Moche ceramics, Paracas tapestries, Chimú gold, and scale models for understanding sights of hard-to-see Chavín and Huari sites.

The museum's most important piece is the Estela Raimondi, a giant stone obelisk that once graced one of Peru's first ceremonial centers, Chavín de Huantár (1300–200 B.C.), near present-day Huaraz. It is carved with snakes, pumas, and the first appearance of the Dios de los Báculos (Staff-Bearing God), which would reappear, in different incarnations, throughout Peru's ancient history. The tour includes a walk through the adjacent colonial home where independence leaders José de San Martín and Simón Bolívar stayed.

Around the corner is the 16th-century Iglesia Magdalena (San Martín and Vivanco, 6:30–8 P.M. Fri.–Tues., 8 A.M.–8 P.M. Thurs.), which has attractive carved altars and a gold painting of Señor de los Tremblores (Lord of the Earthquakes). An excellent restaurant, café, and pisco-tasting bodega, all steeped in tradition, are down the street.

SAN ISIDRO AND MIRAFLORES

What appears to be a clay hill plunked down in the middle of Miraflores is actually a huge adobe pyramid from the Lima culture, which built a dozen major structures in and around what is now Lima A.D. 200–700. **Huaca Pucllana** (General Bolognesi 800, Miraflores, tel. 01/445-8695, http://pucllana.perucultural.org.pe, 9 A.M.–1 P.M. and 1:30–5 P.M. Wed.–Mon., free) has a small but excellent museum, which includes ceramics, textiles, reconstructed tombs, and artifacts from this culture that depended almost entirely on the sea for survival. A recently discovered pot shows a man carrying a shark on his back—proof that this culture somehow hunted 455-kilogram sharks. No free wandering is allowed, but guides lead tours every half hour around the ceremonial plazas and a few inner rooms. This is a good option for those who cannot see the larger Pachacámac, 31 kilometers south of Lima. There is an upscale and delicious restaurant on-site.

A similar, though completely restored, stepped pyramid in San Isidro is **Huaca Huallamarca** (Nicólas de Piérola 201, tel. 01/222-4124, 9 A.M.–5 P.M. Tues.–Sun., US$3.50), which offers a chance to understand what these temples once looked like. From the top, there is an interesting view over Lima's most upscale district.

Museo de Historia Natural (one block west of the 12th block of Arequipa, Arenales 1256, Lince, tel. 01/471-0117, http://museohn.unmsm.edu.pe, 9 A.M.–3 P.M. Mon.–Fri., 9 A.M.–5 P.M. Sat., 9 A.M.–1 P.M. Sun., US$3) is a severely underfunded museum with an aging taxidermy collection that nevertheless offers a good introduction to the fauna of Peru. Many of Peru's top biologists work from here. Ask for permission to see the storage area in the back, where thousands of stuffed birds are archived.

Museo Amano (Retiro 160 near the 11th block of Angamos Oeste, tel. 01/441-2909, tours at 3, 4, and 5 P.M. Mon.–Fri., donations appreciated) has a small but interesting collection of 200 pre-Columbian ceramics, including a Nasca piece with a scene of human sacrifice, and a range of textiles, which are the museum's specialty.

The **Museo Enrico Poli** (Lord Cochrane 466, tel. 01/422-2437 or 01/440-7100,

4–6 P.M., by appointment only, US$12) is one of Lima's more intriguing private collections, with a huge range of textiles, gold and silver objects, and other artifacts. The owner, Enrico Poli, gives the tours personally and speaks Spanish only. Agencies often visit here with their own interpreters.

BARRANCO

This bohemian barrio has a few small museums, the best of which is **Museo Pedro de Osma** (San Pedro de Osma 423, tel. 01/467-

0141, www.museopedrodeosma.org, 10 A.M.–1:30 P.M. and 2:30–6 P.M. Tues.–Sun., US$5), which holds an exquisite private collection of colonial art and furniture. The museum itself is one of Barranco's oldest mansions and is worth a peek just for that reason. Down the street is a small exhibit on electricity in Lima at the **Museo de la Electricidad** (San Pedro de Osma 105, tel. 01/477-6577, http://museo-electri.perucultural.org.pe, 9 A.M.–1 P.M. and 2–5 P.M. Tues.–Sun., free). A restored electric tram, which used to connect Barranco to

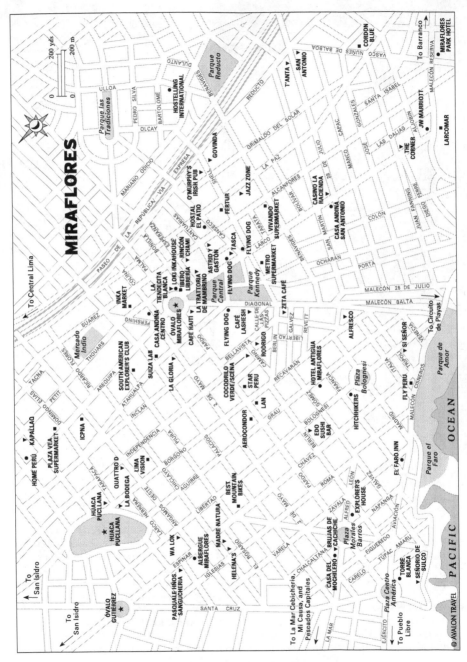

© BETH FUCHS AND JACK HOADLEY

Huaca Pucllana, Miraflores

Miraflores and Lima, runs down the street on Sundays (US$2.75).

EASTERN LIMA
Museo de Oro

Monterrico, an upscale suburb in eastern Lima that is often sunny when the rest of the city is covered in fog, is known for its Museo de Oro (Molina 1110, Monterrico, tel. 01/345-1271, 11:30 A.M.–7 P.M. Mon.–Sun., US$11.50). This fabulous collection of gold pieces was one of Lima's must-see tourist attractions until 2001, when a scandal broke alleging that many of the prize pieces were fakes. Newspapers pointed the finger at the sons of museum founder Miguel Mujica Gallo, whom the newspapers accused of selling the originals and replacing them with imitations. The family countered, saying false pieces were bought by mistake and Mujica Gallo died of sadness in the process. Only true gold pieces are on display now at the museum, but the museum continues to suffer from a credibility problem. Gold pieces include spectacular funerary masks, ceremonial knives

(tumis), a huge set of golden arms, exquisite figurines, and crowns studded with turquoise. It is a huge potpourri of gold, with little explication in English, bought over decades from tomb raiders who work over Moche, Nasca, Sicán, and Chimú sites. Other objects of interest include a Nasca poncho made of parrot feathers and a Moche skull that was fitted, postmortem, with purple quartz teeth. Almost as impressive is the **Arms Museum** upstairs, which is a terrifying assemblage of thousands of weapons, ranging from samurai swords and medieval arquebuses to Hitler paraphernalia.

Museo de la Nación

Peru's largest museum, and cheaper to see than the private collections, is Museo de la Nación (Javier Prado Este 2465, tel. 01/476-9873, 9 A.M.–6 P.M. Tues.–Sun., US$4, US$3 students), in the east Lima suburb of San Borja. Though criticized for a rambling organization, this museum has a great chronological layout, which makes it perhaps Lima's most understandable and educational museum. There are

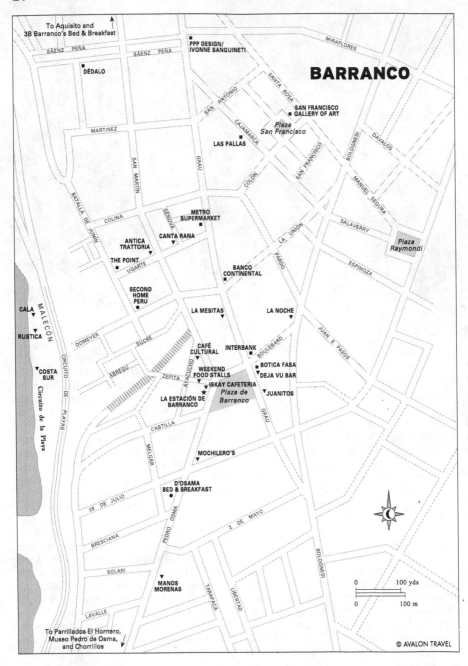

To Aquisito and
3B Barranco's Bed & Breakfast

SÁENZ PEÑA
SÁENZ PEÑA

PPP DESIGN/
IVONNE SANGUINETI

MIRAFLORES

DÉDALO

BARRANCO

SAN ANTONIO

SANTA ROSA

SAN FRANCISCO
GALLERY OF ART

CAJAMARCA

Plaza
San Francisco

MARTINEZ

BOLOGNESI

DÁVALOS

LAS PALLAS

SAN FRANCISCO

GRAU

MANUEL SEGURA

SAN MARTIN

COLÓN

SALAVERRY

BATALLA DE JUNIN

COLINA

SENCIA

METRO
SUPERMARKET

LA UNIÓN

Plaza
Raymondi

ANTICA
TRATTORIA

CANTA RANA

PARDO

ESPINOZA

THE POINT

UGARTE

BANCO
CONTINENTAL

MALECÓN

SECOND
HOME
PERU

CALA

LA MESITAS

LA NOCHE

RUSTICA

DOMEYER

SUCRE

JUAN E PASOS

CIRCUITO

COSTA
SUR

Circuito de la Playa

ABRESU

CAFÉ
CULTURAL

INTERBANK

BOULEVARD

DE

ZEPITA

AYACUCHO

WEEKEND
FOOD STALLS

BOTICA FASA

DEJA VU BAR

PLAYAS

ISKAY CAFETERIA

JUANITOS

LA ESTACIÓN DE
BARRANCO

Plaza de
Barranco

GRAU

CASTILLA

MELGAR

MOCHILERO'S

D'OSAMA
BED & BREAKFAST

PEDRO OSMA

28 DE JULIO

2 DE MAYO

BRESCIANA

BOLOGNESI

SOLARI

MANOS
MORENAS

TARAPACÁ

LIBERTAD

0   100 yds

0   100 m

LAVALLE

To Parrillados El Hornero,
Museo Pedro de Osma,
and Chorrillos

© AVALON TRAVEL

colonial art in Lima's Museo de la Nación

three levels of exhibits showcasing Peru's entire archaeological history, from Chavín stone carvings and Paracas weavings all the way to the Inca. There are good models of Machu Picchu, the Nasca Lines, and the Lords of Sipán tomb excavated near Chiclayo in 1987, one of the great finds of Latin American archaeology. This is a full-blown version of Peru's culture for the history hungry. A more condensed alternative is the Museo Nacional de Arqueología.

OUTSIDE LIMA
Pachacámac
This extensive complex of adobe pyramids, 31 kilometers south of Lima in the Lurín Valley, was the leading pilgrimage center on the central coast and home to the most feared, and respected, oracle in the Andes. The name of Pachacámac in Quechua translates to Lord of the World. Both the Huari and local Inca empires respected the oracle, adding to its prestige with additional buildings and consulting it for important decisions.

During his imprisonment at Cajamarca, Inca Atahualpa complained bitterly because the oracle had falsely predicted he would be victorious against the Spaniards. But Hernando Pizarro was so intrigued by Atahualpa's reports of gold at the oracle that he and a troop of Spanish soldiers rode here from Cajamarca in three weeks. Pushing aside the priests, Pizarro strode to the upmost level of the stepped pyramid. He describes a cane-and-mud house at the top, with a door strangely decorated with turquoise, crystals, and corals. Inside the dark space was a roughly shaped wooden idol. "Seeing the filth and mockery of the idol," Pizarro wrote, "we went out to ask why they thought highly of something so dirty and ugly."

What can be seen today is the idol itself (probably a replica) in the on-site museum and excavations of the main temples and huge pyramids, which have revealed ramps and entranceways. From the top of the Temple of the Sun there is an impressive view of Lima's well-organized shantytown, Villa El Salvador, and the Pacific Coast. The Palacio de Las Mamacuña, the enclosure for holy women built by the Inca, can be seen with

© JORGE RIVEROS CAYO

Pachacámac is an adobe ceromonial complex 31 kilometers south of Lima that was home to an oracle consulted by a series of pre-Colombian cultures in Peru, including the Inca.

a guide only (US$6 for an English-speaking tour of the entire site). On the way to the ruins, you will pass **Reserva Pantanos de Villa** at Km 18 of the Panamericana Sur. There is a surprisingly good range of ducks and other migratory aquatic birds here, luring bird-watchers.

The easiest way to see the ruins and the corresponding museum (http://pachacamac.perucultural.org.pe) is with an agency tour from Lima. Buses marked Pachacámac leave from Montevideo and Ayacucho in central Lima and can be picked up at the Primavera Bridge along the Panamericana Sur (US$4 taxi ride to the bridge from Miraflores). Ask to be dropped off at *las ruinas,* as the town of Pachacámac is farther along.

San Pedro de Casta and Marcahuasi

Marcahuasi is a strange set of rock formations on the high plains above Lima that have attracted a range of theories, from simple wind erosion to the work of UFOs or ancient cultures. The rocks are shaped like people and animals, inspiring names like the Frog, Indian, Three Virgins, and Turtle. Marcahuasi is set amid attractive country scenery and, along with the nearby charming town of San Pedro, makes for a great weekend outing from Lima. To arrive, catch a bus from Avenida Grau in Lima (near Plaza Grau in the center) and travel 1.5 hours to **Chosica,** a resort town 860 meters above sea level that is popular with those trying to escape Lima's fog belt. There are plenty of budget and nicer lodging options here. From Chosica's Parque Echenique, buses leave at 9 A.M. and 3 P.M. to San Pedro, a beautiful four- or five-hour trip that climbs to 3,750 meters above sea level. There is a hostel (US$5 pp) in the main square, along with two restaurants and a tourist information office. Marcahuasi, at 4,100 meters over sea level, is a three-kilometer, 1.5-hour hike; donkeys can be rented for US$6. Entry fee is US$5.

Entertainment and Events

NIGHTLIFE
Central Lima

There are a few night options in the center of Lima, though partakers should take a taxi to and from each one. On the Plaza San Martín is **El Estadio Futbol Club** (Nícolas de Piérola 926, tel. 01/428-8866, www.estadio.com.pe, noon–11 P.M. Mon.–Thurs., noon–3 A.M. Fri.–Sat., noon–5 P.M. Sun.), which is a soccer-lover's paradise bedecked with *fútbol* paraphernalia.

One of the largest and best *peñas* in Lima is **Brisas del Titicaca** (Wakulski 168, near block 1 of Brasil and Plaza Bolognesi, tel. 01/332-1901, www.brisasdeltiticaca.com, Tues.–Sat., US$18 cover). Foreigners come here on Thursday nights for an extraordinary exhibition of dance and music from around Peru that runs 9:30 P.M.–midnight. Those who want to see the same dances, and dance a lot themselves, should come on weekend nights when

mainly Peruvians party 10 P.M.–4 A.M. This is a safe neighborhood and is an easy taxi ride from Miraflores.

San Isidro

If you have come to Avenida Conquistadores for dinner, there are a few nightlife options (which also serve light dinner) along this strip. The moment's favorite spot is **Bravo Restobar** (Conquistadores 1005, tel. 01/221-5700, www.bravorestobar.com, noon–4 P.M. and 7 P.M.–midnight Mon.–Sat., US$15), a swanky wine bar that fills with Lima's hip, 30-something crowd most nights of the week. Another good choice is **Asia de Cuba** (Conquistadores 780, San Isidro, tel. 01/222-4940, www.asiadecubaperu.com), which has an upscale bar and an eclectic after-dinner nightlife scene, including a hookah and blackberry-flavored tobacco in the plush loft.

© ANIBAL SOLIMANO, PROMPERU

Central Lima, long considered unsafe at night by Peruvians and foreigners alike, is making a comeback for travelers looking for affordable accommodations and diverse nightlife.

GAY AND LESBIAN LIMA

Though smaller than that in other Latin American capitals, Lima's gay scene is growing, with a few great new discos and bars. There are a number of websites on gay Peru, but the best and most up-to-date information is on www.lima.queercity.info. This site, written in English, has travel tips, a chat room, links, and an opinionated listing of gay and lesbian bars, discos, saunas, cruising spots, and even retirement options. Other sites include www.peruesgay.com and www.gayperu.com.

A gay-friendly start to the evening is **La Sede** in Miraflores (28 de Julio 441, tel. 01/242-2462, www.publasede.com, 10 P.M.-late Wed.-Sat.).

Gay and lesbian discos do not start swinging until 1 A.M. and continue until the wee hours of the morning. Entry is typically free on weekday nights and goes up after midnight on weekends.

Miraflores's hippest, classiest gay and lesbian disco is **Legendaris** (Berlin 363, www.gayperu.com/legendaris, 11 P.M.-late Wed.-Sun., US$4.50 before midnight, US$6 after), which opened in January 2004 with an extravagant decor, great sound system, and room for 350.

The flamboyant **Downtown Vale Todo** (Pasaje Los Pinos, Miraflores, tel. 01/444-6433, www. peruesgay.com/downtownvaletodo, 10 P.M.-late Wed.-Sun., US$4 Fri.-Sat.) is still open despite some citizens' efforts to shut it down. This disco attracts a younger crowd, with drag queen performances and a cruising bar on an upper deck. The smaller gay disco **Splash** (Pasaje Los Pinos 181, Miraflores, 10:30 P.M. onward Thurs.-Sat.) is on the same street.

A late-2003 addition to San Isidro is **Mercury** (2 de Mayo 1545, tel. 01/592-2340, www.peruesgay.com/downtownvaletodo, 11 P.M.-late Fri.-Sat., US$4.50, US$6 for couples). This disco has two levels, a good music-and-light show, and is in the middle of one of Lima's most fashionable districts.

One of the only options in central Lima is **Sagitario** (Wilson 869, tel. 01/424-4383, www.gayperu.com/sagitariodisco, daily, free except after midnight on weekends), one of Lima's original gay-only bars. The neighborhood is sketchy at night, so travel by taxi.

Avenida 13 (Manuel Segura 270, off block 15 of Arequipa, tel. 01/265-3694) is a gay and lesbian dance club that is **women-only** on Fridays.

Gay-friendly hotels include **Hostal de las Artes** in the center, **Hostel Domeyer** in Barranco, **Aparthotel San Martín** in Miraflores, and **Loft** in San Isidro.

Miraflores

The nightlife in Miraflores is more spread out and harder to find than in the neighboring district of Barranco. And that is precisely why many a traveler ends up at **Calle de las Pizzas** (The Street of the Pizzas), a seedy row of pizza-and-sangria joints right in front of Parque Kennedy. But there are many other options.

If you want a more classic evening head across Parque Kennedy to **Jazz Zone** (La Paz 656, tel. 01/241-8139, http://jazzzoneperu.com, 10 P.M.-2 A.M. Mon.-Sat., free Mon.-Wed., US$7 Thurs., US$11 Fri.-Sat.). Mondays are Afro-Peruvian night, Tuesdays and Wednesdays are Latin jazz, Thursdays bossa nova, and weekends for all of the above.

For cocktails and music, swing around to Francisco de Paula Camino Street to **Cocodrilo Verde** (Francisco de Paula Camino 226, tel. 01/242-7583, www.cocodriloverde.com, 9 P.M.-1 A.M. Thurs.-Sat., free Thurs., US$18 Fri.-Sat.). Next door, **Scena Restaurante** (Francisco Paula de Camino 280, tel. 01/445-9688, www.scena.com.pe, 12:30-4 P.M. and 7:30 P.M.-12:30 A.M. Mon.-Sat., US$10-15) has a great wine list and a rotating art exhibit. **Huaringas** (Bolognesi 460, tel. 01/466-6536, www.brujasdecachiche.com.pe, noon-4:30 P.M. and 7 P.M.-midnight Mon.-Sat., 12:30-4:30 P.M. Sun.) is rumored to have the best pisco sours in town. Get there early, and try the strawberry, passion fruit, and grape sours.

There are several British-style pubs in Miraflores, good for drinking draft ales and playing darts, and the classic is **O'Murphy's Irish Pub** (Schell 627, 6 P.M.–2 A.M. daily), with Guinness on tap, darts, and a pool table. To hang out with an international crowd, there's **Tasca** (Diez Canseco and Parque Kennedy, tel. 01/241-1832, www.flyingdog-peru.com, noon–2 A.M. Mon.–Sat., 5 P.M.–midnight Sun., US$9), a small, tapas-like bar. Or there's **The Corner Sports Bar and Grill** (Larco 1207, tel. 01/444-0220, 11 A.M.–3 A.M. daily, US$8), whose 26 TVs broadcast international sports games.

There is always something happening at **Larcomar** (Malecón de la Reserva 610, www.larcomar.com), the oceanfront mall at the end of Avenida Larco. Even those who dislike malls are impressed with this public space, buried in the cliffside and overlooking the Pacific. Lima's hottest and most expensive new disco, **Aura** (Larcomar 236, tel. 01/242-5516, www.aura.com.pe, 9 P.M.–7 A.M. Thurs.–Sat., cover varies depending on event), is here.

Barranco

The most happening neighborhood for nightlife, any day of the week, is Barranco. **Juanito's** (Grau 274, 11 A.M.–3 A.M. daily, no cover) is a hole-in-the-wall bar that has been a gathering spot for intellectuals since the 1960s. The traditional fare at Juanito's, right on the main square, is malt beer and smoked ham sandwiches. **La Noche** (Bolognesi 307, tel. 01/477-4154, www.lanoche.com.pe, 7 P.M.–3 A.M. daily, US$6–9) is Barranco's best live music bar, with tables set on different levels to look down on a range of (mostly jazz) performances. Monday nights, when there is no cover charge, are especially crowded. **Mochileros** (San Pedro de Osma 135, tel. 01/274-1225, 6 P.M.–2 A.M. daily, no cover), in a 1903 house, has a great patio, with live rock bands and mind-blowing cocktails.

Located in one of Barranco's oldest colonial homes, **Deja Vu Bar** (Grau 294, tel. 01/247-3742, 7 P.M.–2 A.M. Mon.–Sat., no cover) is a dance club for the young and wild.

Barranco is full of *peñas* (live *criollo* music clubs) that make for a rowdy night out among locals. **La Candelaría** (Bolognesi 292, tel. 01/247-2941, www.lacandelariaperu.com, 9:30 P.M.–2 A.M. Fri.–Sat., US$10) is a new and comfortable *peña* where spectators do not stay seated for long. With a slightly older crowd, **La Estación de Barranco** (Pedro de Osma 112, tel. 01/247-0344, 7 P.M.–2 A.M. daily, no cover) is a nice place to hear *música criolla* in the digs of an old train station. The most upscale *peña* in Lima, and a good restaurant, is **Manos Morenas** (Pedro de Osma 409, Barranco, tel. 01/467-0421, www.manosmorenasperu.com, US$16). Shows start at 9 P.M. Tuesday–Thursday, and at 10:30 P.M. Friday–Saturday.

The hippest, but still authentic, *peña* is **Peña del Carajo** (Catalino Miranda 158, tel. 01/247-7023, www.del-carajo.com, 6 P.M.–2 A.M. Fri.–Sat., no cover). Cockfights are waged in the entrance arena and *música negra* plays inside.

CINEMAS

Lima has more cinemas than the rest of the country combined. Most foreign movies are shown in their original language with subtitles, except for children's movies, which are often dubbed. Film listings are posted in *El Comercio* (www.elcomercioperu.com.pe).

The **Centro Cultural PUCP** (Camino Real 1075, tel. 01/616-1616, http://cultural.pucp.edu.pe), in **San Isidro,** hosts several film festivals throughout the year. Its biggest show is in August with the increasingly well-known Lima Latin American Film Festival.

In **Miraflores** alone there are three multiplexes showing both Hollywood and Latin American movies: **Cineplanet Alcázar** (Santa Cruz 814, Óvalo Gutierrez, Miraflores, tel. 01/421-8200, www.cineplanet.com.pe, US$7), **El Pacífico 12** (Jose Pardo 121, Miraflores, tel. 01/445-6990, US$5.50), and **Multicines Larcomar** (in Larcomar mall at end of Larco, tel. 01/446-7336, www.uvkmulticines.com, US$3). A smaller recommended theater is **Cine Club Miraflores** (Larco 770, Miraflores, tel. 01/446-2649). In central Lima there is

Cineplanet Centro (Jr. de la Union 819, tel. 01/428-8460, www.cineplanet.com.pe, US$2, US$3.50 Mon.–Wed.).

For art and classic films, check out **El Cinematógrafo** (Pérez Roca 196, Barranco, tel. 01/477-1961, www.elcinematografo.com, US$4.50) in **Barranco.**

PERFORMING ARTS

For the most up-to-date listing of cultural events, pick up the monthly *Guía del Arte de Lima,* which is available free in most museums and cultural centers. Or view its website, http://guiadelarte.perucultural.org.pe. *El Comercio* (www.elcomercioperu.com.pe) newspaper also has complete listings.

Lima's performing arts received a body blow when the Teatro Municipal, the main venue for ballet, symphony, and opera, burnt to the ground in 1998. Some of these events have been transferred to the **Teatro Segura** (Huancavelica 265, central Lima, tel. 01/426-7189) or the **Museo de la Nación** (Javier Prado Este 2465, San Borja, tel. 01/476-9878).

Theater productions, always in Spanish, can be seen at **Centro Cultural de España** (Natalio Sánchez 181, Sta. Beatriz, www.ccelima.org), **Centro Cultural PUCP** (Camino Real 1075, San Isidro, tel. 01/616-1616, http://cultural. pucp.edu.pe), **Teatro Canout** (Petit Thouars 4550, Miraflores, tel. 01/422-5373), **Teatro Marsano** (General Suárez 409, Miraflores), **Teatro La Plaza Usil** in Larcomar (tel. 01/242-9266, www.larcomar.com), **Alianza Francesa** (Arequipa 4595, tel. 01/241-7014, www.alianzafrancesalima.edu.pe), and **Teatro Británico** (Bellavista 531, Miraflores, tel. 01/447-1135, www.britanico.edu.pe), which occasionally has plays in English. Tickets are normally purchased at the box office for only US$8–12.

Other frequent cultural events, such as films, concerts, and expositions, are held at the **Instituto Cultural Peruano Norteamericano** (tel. 01/706-7000, www.icpna.edu.pe), with a location in central Lima (Cusco 446) and Miraflores (Angamos Oeste 106); the **Centro Cultural Ricardo Palma** (Larco 770, Miraflores, tel. 01/446-3959); and the

Asociación Cultural Peruano Británica (Bellavista 531, Miraflores, tel. 01/447-1135, www.britanico.edu.pe).

CASINOS

Lima is overflowing with casinos, though the most reputable ones tend to be in the major hotels. Wherever you go, do not play the slot machines, as they tend to be rigged. Some casinos open in the evenings and close around dawn. Others are open 24 hours a day. Regardless, they usually offer free drinks, food, and cigarettes to those who are betting.

Better casinos include the **Hotel Sheraton** (Paseo de la República 170, tel. 01/315-5000) in central Lima. In **San Isidro** there's the upscale **Los Delfines Hotel** (Los Eucaliptos 555, tel. 01/215-7000), with minimum US$5 blackjack bets. And in **Miraflores,** the **Stellaris Casino** at the Marriott (Malecón de la Reserva 615, across the street from Larcomar, tel. 01/217-7000) has minimum US$3 bets at the blackjack tables, and Best Western's **Casino la Hacienda** (28 de Julio 511, tel. 01/213-1000) also has a minimum US$3 bet.

SPECTATOR SPORTS

Lima is a great place to catch a **soccer game,** either at the Estadio Nacional along the Vía Expresa and 28 de Julio or at the more modern Estadio Monumental Lolo Fernández in the Molina neighborhood. Games happen mostly on Wednesdays, Saturdays, and Sundays, and prices and locations are published two days beforehand in the newspaper. Tickets run US$5–9 and can usually be bought the same day for nonchampionship matches. Tickets are bought at the stadium, at Farmacia Deza (Conquistadores 1140, San Isidro, tel. 01/222-3195), and at TeleTicket counters at Wong and Metro supermarkets.

Bullfighting takes place at the Plaza de Acho (Hualgayoc 332, tel. 01/481-1467) near the center of Lima from the first week of October to the first week of December, a centuries-old tradition that coincides with Lima's biggest festival, El Señor de los Milagros. Tickets for the Sunday afternoon events range US$30–100 for a two-hour contest featuring world-class bull-fighters from Spain and Peru. Tickets are also sold at Farmacio Deza and at TeleTicket counters in Wong and Metro supermarkets.

Cockfights, traditionally part of *criollo* culture, are weekend events at various *peñas* and the **Coliseo de Gallos Sandia** in Surquillo.

Horse races can be seen at the **Jockey Club of Peru** (El Derby s/n, puerta 3, Hipódromo de Monterrico, tel. 01/610-3000), where betting races are held Tuesdays, Thursdays, and weekends.

To watch American football or European soccer, head to **The Corner Sports Bar and Grill** (Larco 1207, tel. 01/444-0220, 11 A.M.–3 A.M. daily). With TVs even in the bathrooms, you are unlikely to miss a moment of action.

FESTIVALS

Lima's biggest festival is **El Señor de los Milagros** (The Lord of Miracles), which draws as many as a half million people on its main days of October 18 and 28 and is accompanied by bullfights at Plaza de Acho. The processions begin in central Lima at **Iglesia Las Nazarenas** (Tacna and Huancavelica), which was built atop a wall where a black slave painted an image of Christ in the 17th century. The wall was the only thing left standing after a 1755 earthquake, prompting this annual festival in October, the month when Lima's worst earthquakes have traditionally struck. To this day a brotherhood of priests of mainly African descent care for the image, which some anthropologists say is related to the pre-Hispanic cult of Pachacámac.

Other good festivals include **Lima's anniversary** on January 18, the **Feast of the Crosses up San Cristóbal** on May 3, the **Feast of Santa Rosa de Lima** on August 30, and **Día de la Canción Criolla** (Creole Music Day) on October 30, when *peñas* hold a variety of concerts around the city.

Peruvian *paso* horse competitions are held in the Lurín Valley south of Lima and are highly recommended. These include the Peruvian Paso Horse Competition in February, a national competition in Mamacona in April, and the Amancaes competition, also in Mamacona, in July. For more information see the website www.yachay.com.pe/especiales/caballos (Spanish-only).

Shopping

Lima is the clearinghouse for handicrafts produced in places like Huancayo and Ayacucho and sold with a considerable markup. There is a huge range, from cheap tourist-oriented items to boutique shops, but bargaining is always an option. Several American-style malls have been built in Lima, most notably the cliffside Larcomar at the end of Avenida Larco and under the Parque Salazar.

HANDICRAFTS

In **Pueblo Libre,** an excellent crafts markets with a cause is **La Casa de la Mujer Artesana Manuela Ramos** (Juan Pablo Fernandini 1550, 15th block of Brasil, Pueblo Libre, tel. 01/423-8840, www.casadelamujerartesana. com, 9 A.M.–5 P.M. Mon.–Fri.). Proceeds from this market benefit women's programs across Peru.

The largest crafts markets are in **Miraflores** on blocks 52 and 54 on Petit Thouars. Market after market is filled with alpaca clothing, silver jewelry, ceramics, and textiles from all over the country. **Mercado Indio** (Petit Thouars 5245) and **Indian Market** (Petit Thouars 5321) are the best of the lot, with nicely presented stalls and wide selections. Nearby is a **Manos Peruanas** (Plaza Artesanal, Petit Thouars 5411, tel. 01/242-9726, 10:30 A.M.–7:30 P.M. daily), with a contemporary line of handcrafted silver earrings, necklaces, and bracelets. Other huge, cheap crafts markets are **Feria Artesanal** on Avenida Marina on the way to the airport (every taxi knows it) or in central Lima across from Iglesia Santo Domingo, at the intersection of Camaná and Superunda.

Miraflores's other main shopping strips are in the area next to Parque Kennedy that includes La Paz, Schell, and Diez Canseco Streets. The reasonably priced **Hecho a Mano** (Diez Canseco 298) has a high-quality selection of crafts from all parts of Peru, especially Ayacucho. Another plaza at Diez Canseco 380 is filled with jewelry shops, and a wide selection of baby alpaca sweaters can be found at Diez Canseco 378.

For a more upmarket shopping experience, visit the hugely popular **Larcomar** (Malecón de la Reserva 610, www.larcomar.com), an elegant open-air mall dug under Miraflores's Parque Salazar and perched over the ocean. Upscale alpaca clothing stores (the finest of which is **Alpaca 111,** www.alpaca111.com), cafés, a sushi restaurant, bars, a disco, and a 12-screen cinema are just a few of the businesses here. An excellent place for high-quality jewelry, alpaca clothing, textiles, and creative gifts is **Peru ArtCrafts** (Malecón de la Reserva 610, Larcomar, www.peruartcrafts.com).

The most sophisticated range of handicrafts in Lima can be found in **Barranco. Las Pallas** (Cajamarca 212, tel. 01/477-4629, 9 A.M.–7 P.M. Mon.–Sat.) is a high-end gallery with exquisite Amazon textiles, tapestries, and carved gourds from Huancayo, as well as colonial ceramics from Cusco. Prices run US$30–800. Another good option for high-end crafts and art is **Dédalo** (Saenz Pena 295, Barranco, tel. 01/477-0562, 11 A.M.–9 P.M. Tues.–Sun.). Unique art and antiques from all over the world can be found at **San Francisco Gallery of Art** (Plaza San Francisco 208, tel. 01/477-0537, 10:30 A.M.–1:30 P.M. and 3:30–7 P.M. Mon.–Sat.). Expensive gifts, including jewelry and purses, are sold in the courtyard. For Ayacucho crafts, try **Museo-Galería Popular de Ayacucho** (Pedro de Osma 116, tel. 01/246-0599).

Sáenz Peña is the street for contemporary art. There are numerous galleries, whose work is

© PROMPERU

Larcomar is a giant shopping and entertainment complex perched over Lima's coast and smack in the middle of Miraflores, one of the capital's most upscale neighborhoods.

mostly modern and anything from paintings to photography to sculpture. Check out **Lucía de la Puente Galería de Arte** (Sáenz Peña 206, tel. 01/477-9740, www.gluciadelapuente.com), in a large, old mansion, **PPPP Design** (Grau 810, tel. 01/247-7976), or **Yvonne Sanguineti** (Grau 810, tel. 01/477-0519, 11 A.M.–8 P.M. Mon.–Sat.).

CAMPING EQUIPMENT

If you need to buy outdoor gear, you will pay a premium in Peru and your only options are Lima, Huaraz, and Cusco. Varying qualities of white gas, or *bencina blanca*, can be bought at hardware stores across Peru, so test your stove before you depart. Gas canisters are available only at specialty outdoor stores.

Miraflores has several stores: **Alpamayo** (Larco 345, tel. 01/445-1671, 10 A.M.–8 P.M. Mon.–Sat.) sells tents, backpacks, sleeping mats, boots, rock shoes, climbing gear, water filters, MSR stoves, and more. Similar items are found at **Camping Center** (Benavides 1620 Miraflores, tel. 01/242-1779, www.campingperu.com, 10 A.M.–7 P.M. Mon.–Fri., 10 A.M.–1 P.M. Sat.) and **Mountain Worker** (Centro Comercial Camino Real, A-17 in basement, tel. 01/421-2175). **Todo Camping E.I.R.L.** (Angamos Oeste 350, tel. 01/242-1318, 10 A.M.–8 P.M. Mon.–Sat.) also sells more technical equipment like crampons and higher-end fuel stoves.

BOOKSTORES

The best bookstore in central Lima is **El Virrey** (Paseo los Escribanos 115, tel. 01/427-5080, www.elvirrey.com, 10 A.M.–1 P.M. and 1:30–7 P.M. Mon.–Sat.). If you are looking for specialty books in science, history, or sociology, this is the place to find them. The store also has shops in **San Isidro** (Miguel Dasso 141, tel. 01/440-0607, 8 A.M.–8 P.M. daily) and at Larcomar in **Miraflores** (tel. 01/445-6883, noon–9 P.M. daily).

Additionally, there are several bookstores, or *librerías,* in Miraflores with good English and other foreign language sections. Despite its humble door, **SBS** (Angamos Oeste 301, tel. 01/241-8490, www.sbs.com.pe, 8 A.M.–7 P.M. Mon.–Sat.) has the best collection of English-language guidebooks. Its storefront on Parque Kennedy goes by the name **Ibero Librería** (Larco 199, 10 A.M.–8 P.M. daily) and it has an excellent selection of English-language books as well as a helpful staff. **Crisol** (Santa Cruz 816, Óvalo Gutierrez, tel. 01/221-1010, www.crisol.com.pe, 10 A.M.–8 P.M. daily) is a huge, glassy bookshop in the same mall as the Cineplant Alcázar. Other options are **Zeta** (Comandante Espinar 219, tel. 01/446-5139, www.zetabook.com, 10 A.M.–9 P.M. Mon.–Sat., also at Lima airport) and **Delta Bookstore Librería** (Larco 970, tel. 01/445-8825, 10 A.M.–9 P.M. Mon.–Sat., 11 A.M.–6 P.M. Sun.). International newspapers are available from Miraflores street vendors in front of Café Haiti by Parque Kennedy.

Recreation

BIKING

There are great places to go mountain biking within a few hours of Lima, including Pachacámac and the Reserva Nacional de Paracas. Good bike shops in **Miraflores** include **Best Mountainbikes** (Comandante Espinar 320, tel. 01/263-0964, bestint@terra.com.pe) and **Rent-a-Bike** (Marquez de Torre Tagle 107, tel. 01/446-9682), for rentals. **BiciCentro** (Av. San Luis 2906, tel. 01/475-2645), in **San Borja,** is good for repairs and services. **BikeMavil** (Aviación 4021, tel. 01/449-8435, bikemavil@terra.com.pe), in **Surco,** rents bikes and leads excursions.

BIRD-WATCHING

With an early start, there are several doable bird-watching day trips from Lima. **Pantanos de Villa** is a 396-hectare, protected marsh within the Lima city limits. Here, you can see over 130 coastal marsh species, and the area is accessible by public transportation. For guaranteed sightings of the Humboldt penguin, your best option is the **Pucusana** fishing village. Public transportation also covers this route.

An absolutely excellent bird-watching guide and source is Princeton-trained biologist Thomas Valque's *Where to Watch Birds in Peru*, available through the American Audubon Society or www.granperu.com/birdwatchingbook. PromPeru's website (www.perubirdingroutes.com) is also chock-full of good information.

To make your trip more efficient and learn more, you'll probably want to contact a guide. Thomas Valque's company **Gran Perú** (tel. 01/344-1701, www.granperu.com) leads a variety of scheduled tours and can also coordinate day and private trips. Swedish ornithologist Gunnar Engblom's agency **Kolibri Expeditions** (tel. 01/476-5016, www.kolibriexpeditions.com) offers regular weekend expeditions in the Lima area.

BOWLING

There are plenty of lanes at **Cosmic Bowling** (Larcomar, Malecón de la Reserva 610, Miraflores, tel. 01/445-7776, 10 A.M.–1 A.M., US$14/hour), which turns out the light, leaving patrons to aim in the "cosmic light." **Jockey Plaza** (tel. 01/435-9122, 10 A.M.–midnight, US$15 pp) on Javier Prado in Monterrico also has a huge alley.

COOKING

For those familiar with Lima's culinary delights, it should come as no surprise that it hosts a cooking school licensed by **Cordon Bleu** (Nuñez de Balboa 530, Miraflores, tel. 01/242-8222, www.cordonbleuperu.edu.pe, prices vary by course). The various classes include short-term seminars on Peruvian food, international food, and even desserts. Another option is the hotel and restaurant management school **Cenfotur** (Pedro Martinto 320, tel. 01/241-4726, www.cenfotur.com, US$200 per course), whose workshop classes also feature cocktail making and wine-tasting. At either of

The thermal winds rising from the cold Pacific Ocean allow paragliders to spend hours cruising the coastline of Miraflores.

© MICHAEL TWEDDLE

these institutions you will have to make special arrangements for English-speaking classes.

HORSEBACK RIDING

Check out **Cabalgatas** (tel. 01/9837-5813, www.cabalgatas.com.pe, US$45–65), an option for riding Peruvian *paso* horses near Mamacona, the town where the *paso* horse competitions are held each year. They lead interesting excursions around the ceremonial center of Pachacámac.

PARAGLIDING

First-time visitors to Miraflores, promenading the *malecón*, are sometimes surprised to find a paraglider just meters above their heads, zipping back and forth along the oceanfront bluffs. Although the thrill is short lived, paragliding does offer an excellent alternative viewpoint of Lima. One recommended operator is **Peru Fly** (Jorge Chávez 658, Miraflores, tel. 01/444-5004, www.perufly.com) organizes flights in Lima and Paracas and also offers six-day basic-training courses.

ROCK-CLIMBING WALLS

Available on Mondays, Wednesdays, and Fridays at 7:30 P.M., the rock wall at **Millennium Gym** (Jr. Independencia 145, Miraflores, tel. 01/242-8557) is good training for the boulders around Huaraz. You must become a member to climb. **Youth Hostal Malka** (Los Lirios 165, San Isidro, tel. 01/442-0162, www.youthhostelperu.com) in San Isidro also has a rock wall.

SCUBA

There are no coral reefs on Peru's Pacific coast, but agencies do offer interesting dives. **AguaSport** (Conquistadores 805, San Isidro, tel. 01/221-1548, www.aquasportperu.com) rents all equipment for snorkeling and scuba diving. Standard scuba day trips from Lima include a 30-meter wall dive at Pucusana, an 18-meter dive to a nearby sunken ship, or diving with sea lions at Islas Palomino off Lima. Two dives are US$95, or US$55 if you have your own equipment. This agency rents a range of aquatic and off-road equipment.

SEA KAYAKING

For those who like to get out on the water but aren't surfers, there's always sea kayaking. **Chingos** (tel. 01/9926-6363, www.chingos. com, around US$75 pp) is a professionally run operation, with new equipment, that takes passengers out on the Pacific anywhere between Ancón and Cerro Azul.

SURFING

Though the swells in front of Lima are dotted with dozens of surfers, we do not recommend surfing in these polluted waters. The better breaks are La Herradura in Chorrillos, Punta Hermosa, and Punta Rocas. Or head instead to the beaches north or south of Lima, and you will find some untouched. Keep an eye out for opportunities to surf at **San Gallán**, one of Peru's few right point breaks in the Paracas National Reserve; **Pepinos** and **Cerro Azul,** near the mouth of the Cañete River Valley; and **Playa Grande,** north of Lima, which is a challenging, hollow point break for expert surfers.

Good sources of surfing information are www.surfingperu.org and www.peruazul.com.

For surfing classes, call Rocio Larrañaga at **Surf School** (tel. 01/264-5100 or 01/9710-7345), who will pick you up at your hotel and lend you a wetsuit and board. **Luis Miguel de la Rosa** (tel. 01/9810-1988) offers a similar service. If you're just looking to rent, **Centro Comercial** (Caminos del Inca Tienda 158, Surco, tel. 01/372-5106) has both surfboards and skateboards. **Big Head** (Larcomar, Malecón de la Reserva 610, tel. 01/242-8123) sells new surfboards and body boards along with wetsuits. One of the better surf shops in Peru is **Focus** (Las Palmeras Block C, Playa Arica, Panamericana Sur Km 41, tel. 01/430-0444). The staff is knowledgeable about local surfing spots, rents boards at a good price, and even has a few hostel rooms.

OFF-THE-WALL FUN

Laser tag pickup battles are available at the Jockey Club's **Daytona Park** (El Derby s/n, Puerto 4, Hipódromo de Monterrico, Surco, tel. 01/435-6058, 10 A.M.–10 P.M. daily) and cost US$9 for 30 minutes. It is also possible to go-kart around a racetrack.

Bus Parrandero (Benavides 330, Of. 101, Miraflores, tel. 01/445-4755, www.elbusparrandero.com) operates an air-conditioned **party bus,** where people hop on board, drink as much as they want, and listen to live performers—all for US$25. The bus travels from Miraflores to Plaza Mayor in central Lima and then takes passengers to the popular Barranco *peña* La Candelaría (entry included).

TOUR AGENCIES AND GUIDES

Do not get hustled by agency reps at Lima's airport or bus stations. They will arrange travel packages that tend to be as expensive as, or more expensive than, if you were to do it on your own.

Sightseeing Agencies

Our favorite travel agency in Lima is **Fertur Peru** (www.fertur-travel.com, 8:30 A.M.–8 P.M. Mon.–Sat.), run by the enterprising Siduith Ferrer with offices in central Lima at the Plaza Mayor (Junín 211, tel. 01/427-2626) and Miraflores (Schell 485, tel. 01/242-1900). It can buy a variety of bus and plane tickets and set up tours around Lima and day tours to see Paracas or the Nasca Lines.

Peru's most reputable agency, with decades in business, is **Lima Tours,** with offices in central Lima (Belén 1040, tel. 01/619-6900, www.limatours.com.pe). Its city tours have exclusive access to the pristine 17th-century mansion Casa de Aliaga. Because the company works with large international groups, it is best to get in touch before arrival in Lima.

A good agency for booking flights and other logistics is **Nuevo Mundo,** with offices

in the center (Camaná 782, tel. 01/427-0635), Miraflores (Jorge Chávez 225), and San Isidro (28 de Julio 1120, tel. 01/610-8080).

Reputable agencies in Miraflores include **Exprinter** (Pardo 384, tel. 01/444-5350, www.exprinterviajes.com.pe) and **Carlson Wagonlit Travel** (Ricardo Palma 355, tel. 01/610-1600, www.cwtvacaciones.com.pe).

A final option for day tours in Lima is **Peru Smile** (tel. 01/997-1349, perusmile@yahoo.com), which is run by Jorge Fernández and has tours and prices similar to Lima Vision (but without the large groups).

Many of the recommended agencies sell tours run by **Lima Vision** (Chiclayo 444, Miraflores, tel. 01/447-7710, 24 hours, www.limavision.com), the city's standard pool service, which offers three- to four-hour daily tours of Lima's center (US$25), museums (US$35), Pachacámac (US$35), Museo de Oro (US$25), or a full-day city tour with lunch (US$70). Whether you buy from Lima Vision or from an agency, the cost is the same. All of Peru's main agencies are based in Lima.

Specialized Agencies

For those who can't make it to Paracas, **Ecocruceros** (Arequipa 4960, tel. 01/9910-8396, www.ecocruceros.com) offers half-day boat tours from the port of Callao to see sea lions at the Islas Palomino.

Guides

Recommended and certified private tour guides are **Tino Guzmán Khan** (tel. 01/429-5779, tinogpc@yahoo.com), who speaks English, Chinese, and French, and **Cecilia Paredes** (tel. 01/475-3829), who speaks English, Spanish, and Italian.

Accommodations

When in Lima, our favorite places to stay are Barranco, with lots of nightlife, backpacker options, and bohemian energy, and Miraflores, which has Peru's best selection of hotels and restaurants in all categories. If you're in town for corporate work, or want the highest-end hotels Lima has to offer, San Isidro's financial district is your best bet. If you are comfortable in noisy, developing-world cities and interested in understanding the city's colonial center, you should stay in downtown Lima. The neighborhood of Breña is a more peaceful alternative to the center that is close to the Museo de Arte and a 10-minute walk to the edge of old town. Pueblo Libre, only a 10-minute taxi ride to the center, has a charming small-town feel for those who want to get off the beaten track.

CENTRAL LIMA AND PUEBLO LIBRE
US$10-25

In downtown Lima, the (**Hostal Roma** (Ica 326, tel. 01/427-7576, www.hostalroma.8m. com, US$16 s, US$25 d with breakfast and private bath) is a charming place catering to backpackers. With high ceilings, wood floors, and 10 different types of breakfast, Roma stands out from the rest. Internet, safety boxes, and airport transfers are available. A small, attached café serves espresso, beer, and cocktails. The 36 rooms here fill up fast, so make reservations early.

Another good budget option in downtown Lima is **Hostal España** (Azángaro 105, tel. 01/428-5546, www.hotelespanaperu.com, US$6 dorm, US$12–16 s, US$16–20 d, rooms with private baths US$5 extra). This backpacker classic is a labyrinth of tight halls and patios, decorated with hanging ivy, marble busts, and reproductions of colonial paintings. The rooms are small and basic with clean, shared bathrooms and hot water. Despite its location, the hostel manages to disconnect itself from the hustle and be a peaceful escape. With

One of the best lodging values in all of Lima is the elegant Hostal España, in central Lima.

a charming upstairs restaurant and neighboring Internet café, this place fills up quickly. Make reservations early.

In Breña, the friendly **Hostal Iquique** (Iquique 758, tel. 01/433-4724 or 01/423-3699, www.hostal-iquique-lima.com, US$17 s, US$26 d with breakfast) is a longtime backpackers' favorite with good service, kitchen, rooftop terrace, and hot water. Rooms with tiled floors are not too noisy and some even have TVs. Private baths cost an additional US$4–7.

Bordering Breña, **Hostal de Las Artes** (Chota 1460, tel. 01/433-0031, www.hostaldelasartes.net, US$5 for dorm bed, US$9 s, US$18 d) is a clean, well-managed, gay-friendly place with Dutch owners. Sevillean-style tiles line the entrance off a quiet street that is a 10-minute walk from Plaza San Martín. Rooms are simple with whitewashed walls, dark wood, comfy beds, and near silence. A book exchange, gardens, and two patios round out the hostel. There are good restaurants down the street.

Pueblo Libre's artist-owned **Guest House Marfil** (Parque Ayacucho 126, tel. 01/463-3161, casamarfil@yahoo.com, US$12 s, US$18 d) is a converted house with splashes of color, lots of paintings on the walls, and three resident cats. The bohemian rooms are private, making this a great value, and the shared baths are clean with plenty of hot water. There are two Internet stations and a group kitchen. Banks and supermarkets are nearby.

US$25-50

Sitting at the end of a quiet park, near the Museo de Arte, is the recommended **Posada del Parque** (Parque Hernán Velarde 60, block 1 Petit Thouars, tel. 01/433-2412, www.incacountry.com, US$31 s, US$41 d). This hotel in an old colonial house, filled with traditional art, is the perfect escape from central Lima. The Parque de la Exposición, just blocks away, makes for great strolling. Monica, the attentive owner, provides two Internet-ready computers, firm beds, great "what to do" advice, and a sitting room with a TV and DVD player.

Hostal Bonbini (Cailloma 209, tel. 01/427-6477, http://bonbini.tripod.com.pe, US$30 s, US$40 d with breakfast) has large rooms with nice but dated furniture, cable TV, and big bathrooms. Avoid noisy rooms on the street front. **Hotel Kamana** (Camaná 547, tel. 01/427-7106, www.hotelkamana.com, US$43 s, US$58 d with breakfast) is overpriced, but safe and well operated. There is a 24-hour snack bar, and the back rooms are quiet. This is a safe and reliable option for a good night's sleep.

Over US$150

The only five-star hotel in central Lima is the **Hotel Sheraton** (Paseo de la República 170, tel. 01/315-5000, www.sheraton.com. pe, US$165 s, US$190 d), a square tower that rises at the entrance to old town. This business hotel has a huge open atrium rising 19 floors. The normal rooms have older furniture and feel four-starish. If you stay here, upgrade to the tower rooms on the upper floors, which have easy chairs, California king-size beds, elegant wood floors and paneling, and astounding views over Lima. Other services include whirlpool tub, sauna, gym, and ground-floor casino. If you bargain, prices at this hotel get as low as US$83.

SAN ISIDRO
US$10-25

The bulk of San Isidro's hotels are oriented toward high-class business travelers, but there is one great exception to this rule. **Youth Hostal Malka** (Los Lirios 165, San Isidro, tel. 01/442-0162, www.youthhostelperu.com, US$8 dorm, US$19 d) is a rare find with its own rock-climbing wall. This converted home has simple, clean rooms, Internet, laundry service, and a grassy yard with a table tennis table. The hostel is a block from a park, and a supermarket and a few restaurants are down the street. Rooms with private baths are US$2 more.

US$100-150

Like its sister hotels around the country, **Hotel Libertador San Isidro Golf** (Los Eucaliptos 550, San Isidro, tel. 01/421-6666 or U.S.

tel. 800/537-8483, www.libertador.com.pe, US$115 s or d with breakfast) is an elegant, classy act. These four-star rooms are a great value, with dark-stained furniture, elegant carpets, golf course views, and all the creature comforts, including luxurious bathrooms with tubs. There is an elegant pub downstairs with lots of wood, and the Ostrich House Restaurant serves up ostrich and other delicious steaks. Features include a sauna, whirlpool tub, and gymnasium.

Over US$150

At the top of El Olívar, a park shaded by ancient olive trees, **Sonesta Hotel El Olivar** (Pancho Fierro 194, San Isidro, tel. 01/712-6000, www.sonesta.com, US$230 s, US$260 d with breakfast) has spacious though quite ordinary rooms, a beautiful sitting area with bar, and a rooftop pool. Ask for a room with views over the olive grove.

Built in 1927, the **Country Club Lima Hotel** (Los Eucaliptos 590, San Isidro, www.hotelcountry.com, US$295 s, US$310 d) has a classic, turn-of-the-20th-century elegance. Couches fill a marble lobby decorated with Oriental rugs, dark wood, and high windows. Perks include an elegant restaurant, an English bar, a gymnasium, and an outdoor pool. Suites are decorated with museum pieces from Museo de Osma. Ask for a room with a balcony or a view over the golf course, which as a guest you'll be able to play.

Sandwiched between the Camino Real Mall and a glassy office park, **Swissôtel** (Via Central 150, San Isidro, tel. 01/421-4400 or U.S. tel. 800/637-9477, www.swissotel-lima.com, US$330 s or d with breakfast) is one of Peru's leading business hotels. All rooms have king-size beds, down comforters, large bathrooms with tubs, and wireless Internet. Each floor has its own security card. You have your choice of food: Swiss, Italian, or Peruvian. An elegant swimming pool surrounded by grassy lawn, a tennis court, a whirlpool tub, a sauna, and a gym make for a relaxing afternoon.

Los Delfines (Los Eucaliptos 555, tel. 01/215-7000, www.losdelfineshotel.com,

US$219 s or d, buffet breakfast included), with a pool full of leaping dolphins, was an extravagant concept from the go-go Fujimori years. But guests eating breakfast or having a drink at the bar seem to love the hotel pets: dolphins. The comfortable rooms feel new and are decked out with deep blue carpets, elegant tables, and bathrooms. Amenities include a casino, luxurious outdoor pool, spa with massages, aerobics room, sauna, and whirlpool tub, and the restaurant serves first-class Mediterranean food.

An upcoming luxury hotel, which will likely become Lima's most expensive hotel, is **Westin Libertador** (tel. 01/421-6666 or U.S. tel. 800/537-8483, www.libertador.com.pe, US$300 s or d with breakfast). This 301-room skyscraper, right in the middle of San Isidro's financial district, is set to open in 2011 with two restaurants, a bar-lounge, luxury spa, and conference facility.

Long-Term Stays

With a minimum stay of 15 days, **Loft** (Jorge Basadre 255, Of. 202, tel. 01/222-8983, www.loftapar.com), an apartment rental agency, offers travelers well-located, fully equipped apartments in San Isidro and Miraflores. Rates start at US$500 a month for the studio but there are also one-, two-, and three-bedroom apartments.

MIRAFLORES

Along with San Isidro, Miraflores is one of Lima's upscale districts. The shopping and restaurants are top-notch, and you're only a five-minute cab ride to nightlife action in Barranco.

US$10-25

One of the best places in town to meet other travelers is **Home Peru** (Arequipa 4501, tel. 01/241-9898, www.homeperu.com, US$9 dorm, US$12 pp s, US$24 d shared bath with breakfast), a restored colonial mansion five blocks from Miraflores's Parque Kennedy. Spacious, sunny wood-floored rooms have comfortable bunk beds and shared baths with hot water. There is a nice room on the ground floor with cable TV, as well as free Internet, inexpensive laundry, a shared kitchen (the supermarket is just a block away!), and a charming open-air dining area for morning breakfasts.

A great place for budget travelers is **Explorer's House** (Alfredo León 158, tel. 01/241-5002, explorers_house@yahoo.es, US$8 dorm, US$12 s, US$20 d with breakfast). The house-cum-hostel has a common kitchen and TV room with a video library. The communal baths are clean, and laundry is US$1/kilogram. The friendly owners Maria Jesus and Victor give a remembrance gift upon departure!

Casa del Mochilero (Cesareo Chacaltana 130A, 2nd Fl., tel. 01/444-9089, juan_kalua@hotmail.com, US$8 pp dorm with shared bath) is a clean and plain backpackers' hangout, about 10 minutes' walk from Parque Kennedy, with bunk rooms, shared bathrooms, and group kitchen. Mochilero's Inn is a lesser, though similarly priced, knockoff down the street, which we do not recommend.

Loki Inkahouse (Larco 189, tel. 01/242-4350, www.lokihostel.com, US$8 dorm, US$24 s, US$25 d with breakfast), on Parque Kennedy, couldn't be better located. Next door are some of the city's busiest restaurants and bars. But you may never need to visit them. Loki's Peruvian owners have converted this colonial house into a backpacker's haven, with everything you might want: a great rooftop patio, card-playing tables, three Internet stations, a TV/DVD room, a communal kitchen, and even a bar.

It doesn't get more secure than at **Hitchhikers** (Bolognesi 400, tel. 01/242-3008, www.hhikersperu.com, US$10 dorm, US$25 s and d with breakfast), an old house tucked away behind fortress-like walls. There's no scrimping on space here. Shared rooms have tall ceilings, the communal kitchen has two rooms, and there's even a huge parking area, which doubles as a table tennis arena.

The cheerful **Flying Dog Hostels** (www.flyingdogperu.com, US$10 dorm, US$23 d with breakfast) have become an institution in central Miraflores, and there are locations in other parts of Peru. The three Lima locations (Diez Canseco 117, tel. 01/445-0940; Lima 457, tel. 01/444-5753; Martir Olaya 280, tel. 01/447-0673) are within a stone's throw of Parque Kennedy, and all guests eat breakfast at outdoor cafés on the park. The layout of each hostel is more or less the same: tight dormitory rooms, a few private rooms, sitting areas, clean bathrooms, and lots of hot water. If you make a reservation, be sure to know for which Flying Dog you've made it. They also have options for longer stays.

Hostelling International (Casimiro Ulloa 328, tel. 01/446-5488, www.limahostell.com. pe, US$12 dorm, US$18 s, US$24 d) has a variety of rooms spread out in an old home with sunny courtyard that is a 10-minute walk to Parque Kennedy. There is a travel agency in the lobby.

US$25-50

The charming **Hostal El Patio** (Diez Canseco 341, tel. 01/444-2107, www.hostalelpatio.net, US$40 s, US$50 d with breakfast) is a memorable colonial home overflowing with plants and flowers and cheerfully painted walls. Large rooms have either tiled floors or carpet, as well as homey furnishings and large windows. Ask for a mini-suite for an additional US$5—you'll get your money's worth with a kitchenette. Rooms are interspersed with terraces, which are great places for reading or sunbathing.

Francis, the friendly owner of **Albergue Miraflores** (Espinar 611, tel. 01/447-7748, www.alberguemirafloreshouse.com, US$34 d or s with breakfast), claims that his second-floor staircase is practice for Machu Picchu. Then he laughs. It is the cheerful attitude that makes the small, dark rooms acceptable. Plus there are spacious common rooms, Internet, a patio with a barbecue, and third-floor rooms with nice lighting.

US$50-100

Our favorite upscale hotel in Lima is the charming **Hotel Antigua Miraflores** (Grau 350, tel. 01/241-6166, www.peru-hotels-inns. com, US$79 s, US$94 d with breakfast). This turn-of-the-20th-century mansion has all the comforts of a fine hotel and the warmth of a bed-and-breakfast. The rooms are large, cozy, and handsomely decorated with hand-carved furniture, local art, and warm colors. Plus, the remodeled bathrooms have big tubs. There are plush couches in the downstairs sitting room, and the six types of breakfast are served in a sunny, black-and-white-tiled café. It is worth paying another US$20 for a room in the old part of the house, and suites are also available with kitchens and whirl-pool tubs.

Across the street from the handicrafts-haven Inka Market, the new, upscale **Casa Andina Centro** (Petit Thouars 5444, tel. 01/447-0263, www.casa-andina.com, US$65 s, US$80 d with breakfast) puts you in the middle of the action, but without the hustle. Rooms have everything for comfort: modern bathrooms, firm beds, down comforters, cable TV, minifridges, air-conditioning, and Internet in the lobby. The hotel chain has a second location slightly away from the center, **Casa Andina San Antonio** (Av. 28 de Julio 1088, tel. 01/241-4050), which is near some of Miraflores's best cafés, and another five-star version nearby as well.

Aparthotel San Martín (San Martín 598, tel. 01/242-0500, www.sanmartinhotel.com, US$110 s, US$130 d) offers spacious suites with living room, double bedroom, closet, bathroom, kitchen, cable TV, and phone. There are beds for two people and a pullout couch for two more. Floors 8–10 have wireless Internet.

The new **El Faro Inn** (Francia 857, tel. 01/242-0339, www.elfaroinn.com, US$40 s, US$60 d with breakfast) is a modern hotel one block from the oceanfront. Small rooms are carpeted, with cable TV and basic furnishings. Other amenities include cheap Internet, laundry, and a rooftop terrace. Also one block from the oceanfront is **Hostal Torre Blanca** (José Pardo 1453, tel. 01/242-1876, www.torreblancaperu.com, US$53 s, US$65 d with breakfast), which offers large carpeted rooms with cable TV and minifridge. There is free Internet and airport transfer.

Over US$150

Most of the five-star hotels are in San Isidro, but Lima's best is **Miraflores Park Hotel** (Malecón de la Reserva 1035, tel. 01/610-4000, www.mira-park.com, from US$230 s or d). This elegant glass high-rise, located on an old park overlooking the ocean, offers the best in service, comfort, and views in Lima. The grand marble entry is decorated with antique furnishings that are complemented by modern art. The luxurious rooms offer ocean views, elegant furnishings, cable TV with DVD player, fax machines, and wireless Internet. Other amenities include video library, massage (US$40), swimming pool, and squash court.

The oceanfront **JW Marriott** (Malecón de la Reserva 615, tel. 01/217-7000, www.marriotthotels.com, US$245 s, US$265 d) occupies prime real estate overlooking the Pacific Ocean and just across the street from the deluxe, full-service Larcomar mall. The rooms live up to five-star Marriott quality and are nearly silent despite the street below. For the best view, ask for a room on one of the upper floors with ocean view. Perks include glass-enclosed bars and restaurants, casino, pool, and tennis court.

BARRANCO
US$10-25

The Point (Malecón Junín 300, tel. 01/247-7997, www.thepointhostels.com, US$9–11 dorm, US$15 s, US$22 d with breakfast) is a backpacker option with everything a traveler needs: WiFi, long-distance calling, sitting room with cable TV, nice bunk beds with shared bathrooms, cheap lunches, pool table, sauna, book exchange, travel agency, a grassy lawn, and an outdoor bar. This 11-room, restored 19th-century house is just paces away from Barranco's best bars and sweeping ocean views. There are frequent barbecues and Monday night outings to the local jazz bar, La Noche.

US$25-50

D'Osma Bed & Breakfast (Pedro de Osma 240, tel. 01/251-4178, www.deosma.com,

US$22–40 s, US$30–50 d with breakfast) has upgraded its services and is a great option if you are looking for a tranquil, family-oriented environment.

Backpackers Inn (Malecón Castilla 260, tel. 01/247-3709, backpackersinnperu@hotmail. com, US$10–11 dorm, US$30 d with breakfast) is another option, less hectic and more quiet. Some rooms open onto the oceanfront, and a nearby path leads down to the beach. The inn has a communal kitchen, sofa lounge, dining room with board games, TV and DVD player, WiFi, and plenty of tourist information.

Aquisito (Centenario 114, tel. 01/247-0712, US$18 s, U$29 d) is a great bed-and-breakfast. The place is small and cozy, located on a noisy part of Barranco but incredibly quite inside. Rooms are comfortable and staff are quite friendly and helpful.

US$50-100

3B Barranco's Bed & Breakfast (Centenario 130, tel. 01/247-6915, www.3bhostal.com, US$55 s and d) is the newest addition to a group of comfy and well-equipped hostels and bed-and-breakfasts in Barranco. With a neat, minimalistic design and decor, the rooms are clean, bright, and spacious with very comfy beds and impeccable bathrooms. The hostel is on a very busy street but two blocks away from the ocean and a few more from all of Barranco's nightlife.

Second Home Peru (Domeyer 366, tel. 01/477-5021, www.secondhomeperu.com, US$75 s, US$85 d with breakfast) is inside the home of Víctor Delfin, a prominent Peruvian painter and sculptor, and his works fill the first floor of the house as well as the five elegant guest rooms. Lilian Delfin, his daughter, is a welcoming and helpful host who will lead you into a morning visit to Víctor's studio. A swim in the cool pool overlooking the ocean from a cliff, with a lion fountain spouting above, is an absolute must. The high ceilings, crisp white linens, and designer bathrooms make any visitor to Second Home feel simultaneously at ease and re-fined. All rooms have cable Internet connection. A night in this hotel should not be missed.

Food

Peruvian cuisine has an extraordinary range of flavors and ingredients, and nowhere is that more evident than Lima. The range of high-quality restaurants is extraordinary. The best lunch deal is always the fixed-price *menú*, which typically includes three well-prepared courses. Upscale restaurants tack on a 10 percent service charge and an 18 percent value-added tax.

The center has good budget eateries, including some of the best *chifa* (Chinese-Peruvian food) in town. San Isidro and Miraflores have the most interesting and refined restaurants, where dozens of Cordon Bleu–trained chefs busily cater to their refined Lima clientele.

CENTRAL LIMA AND PUEBLO LIBRE

Other than the cluster of restaurants around Pasaje Nicolás de Ribera El Viejo and Pasaje Santa Rosa, central Lima's restaurants are spread out. That said, it is worth taking a cab to some of them, especially the classics in Pueblo Libre.

Cafés, Bakeries, and Ice Cream

Antigua Taberna Queirolo (San Martín 1090, tel. 01/460-0441, www.antiguataber-naqueirolo.com, 10 A.M.–10 P.M. daily, US$8) is a charming Spanish-style café that has been open since 1880. This is a good place to come in the afternoon or evenings to sample pisco (fortified wine), made in the winery next door. There is a slim but good menu that includes salted ham sandwiches, plates of sausage, and steamed fish.

Opening onto the lawns of the Museo Larco is the tasteful **Café del Museo** (Bolívar 1515, tel. 01/462-4757, www.museolarco.org,

A baking contest in Lima features such delights as *budín de durazno* (peach pudding).

9 A.M.–6 P.M. daily, US$10). Renato Peralta leads the small kitchen and sends out precisely flavored, light plates of ceviche, *rocoto relleno*, and *chicharrones*.

Sandwiches and salads, as well as truffles, cakes, and mousses, are available at **Cocolat Café** (Pasaje Nicolas de Rivera el Viejo 121, tel. 01/427-4471, 8 A.M.–6:30 P.M. daily, US$4–7). Nearby is the historic **El Cordano** (Ancash 202, tel. 01/427-0181, 8 A.M.–9 P.M. daily, US$6–12), a century-old establishment that was a favored haunt of writers and intellectuals. Though its facade is a bit tattered, this is an excellent place to come for a US$3 pisco sour or a filling midday meal.

Peruvian

If you are staying in Pueblo Libre or visiting the Museo Larco, eat lunch in the neighborhood. **El Bolivariano** (Pasaje Santa Rosa 291, tel. 01/261-9565, www.elbolivariano.com, 10 A.M.–10 P.M. daily, US$10) is a time-honored Lima restaurant in an elegant republican-style home that is visited mainly by Peruvians. The menu includes Peruvian classics such as

seco de cabrito (stewed goat) and *arroz con pato* (rice with duck). More intimate than its sister restaurant in Breña, **La Choza Náutica** (La Mar 635, tel. 01/261-5537, www.lachozanautica.com, 10 A.M.–8 P.M. daily) has excellent ceviche and seafood.

OK, it is a chain, but **Pardo's** (Pasaje Santa Rosa 153, tel. 01/427-2301, www.pardoschicken.com.pe, noon–11 P.M. daily, US$10–12) still serves the best spit-roasted chicken, with affordable lunch menus and open-air tables right off the Plaza Mayor. It also serves *anticuchos*, brochettes, and *chicharrones*.

In the same pedestrian walkway, **T'anta** (Pasaje Nicolás de Rivera el Viejo 142-148, tel. 01/428-3115, 9 A.M.–9 P.M. Mon.–Sat., 9 A.M.–6 P.M. Sun., US$7–14), a Gaston Acurio restaurant, serves up refined plates of Peruvian favorites *lomo saltado* and *recoto relleno*, as well as creative new inventions like *ají de gallina* ravioli.

A new and more upscale spot is **Los Virtrales de Gemma** (Ucayali 332, tel. 01/426-7796, 9 A.M.–7 P.M. Mon.–Sat., US$10), in a restored colonial home one block

© JORGE RIVEROS CAYO

A bartender at Malabar serves up a pisco sour.

from the Plaza Mayor. The hardworking owners have created an excellent and varied menu of Peruvian and international food.

Though a bit faded from its past glory, **L'Eau Vive** (Ucayali 370, tel. 01/427-5612, 12:30–3 P.M. and 7:30–9:30 P.M. Mon.–Sat., US$7) still serves up wholesome and delicious lunch *menús* prepared by a French order of nuns. Dinners feature cocktails, the singing of "Ave María," and an eclectic selection of international entrées.

In Breña, **La Choza Náutica** (Breña 204, off first block of Arica, tel. 01/423-8087, www.lachozanautica.com, 11 A.M.–1 A.M., US$9–11) is a former hole-in-the-wall *cebichería* that has become more upscale and successful over the years. It serves special ceviches (including an "erotic" version) and *tiraditos* in huge portions.

Chifa

When in central Lima, do not miss the opportunity to sample *chifa* (Chinese-Peruvian cuisine) at one of the largest Chinatowns in South America. There are at least a dozen places spread along the town's two main streets, Capón and Paruro. The best known of Lima's Chinatown is **Wa Lok** (Paruro 864, tel. 01/427-2750, 9 A.M.–11 P.M. daily, US$12–17), serving more than 20 types of dim sum. Try *ja kao dim sum,* a mixture of pork and shrimp with rice, or *siu mai de chanco,* shredded pork with mushroom and egg pasta. A good, less expensive alternative to Wa Lok, with a more elegant dining room, is **Salon Capon** (Paruro 819, tel. 01/426-9286, 9 A.M.–11 P.M. Mon.–Sat., US$8–10), serving Peking duck, *langostinos Szechuan* (sautéed shrimps with *ají*), and *chuleta kin tou* (grilled sweet pork). Both have lovely display cases of after-lunch desserts.

Vegetarian

The Hare Krishna–operated **Govinda** (Callao 480, tel. 01/426-1956, 9:30 A.M.–9 P.M. Mon.–Sat.), the country's tried-and-true vegetarian chain, has a varied, inventive menu with pizzas, sandwiches, yogurts, and veggie Chinese food.

SAN ISIDRO

San Isidro's restaurant and nightlife scene lives mostly on the Avenida de los Conquistadores.

Here, you will find some of Lima's newest and most upscale restaurants.

Cafés, Bakeries, and Ice Cream

For those who want a good place to read, **La Baguette** (Aliaga 456, 7 A.M.–11 P.M. Sun.–Wed., 7 A.M.–midnight Thurs.–Sat., US$7) has a nice second-story balcony and a long list of sandwiches on real baguettes. **Don Mamino** (Conquistadores 790, tel. 01/344-4004, 6:30 A.M.–11 P.M. daily) has gourmet desserts and fresh-baked breads. **The Ice Cream Factory** (Conquistadores 395, tel. 01/222-2633, 11 A.M.–10 P.M. daily) has a good range of ice creams and affordable sandwiches. The geranium-lined patio of **La Bonbonneire** (Burgos 415, tel. 01/421-2447, 8 A.M.–midnight Tues.–Sun., US$9) is straight out of France, as are the delicate sandwiches of cream cheese and smoked trout. The patio of **T'anta** (Pancho Fierro 117, tel. 01/421-9708, US$7–14) is an excellent place to linger over a cup of coffee, glass of wine, or a rich chocolate dessert. The very best ice cream in Peru is at **Quattro D** (Las Begonias 580). *Lúcuma* and chocolate make an unbeatable double scoop.

Peruvian

Punta Sal (Conquistadores 948, tel. 01/441-7431, www.puntasal.com, 11 A.M.–5 P.M. daily, US$10–14) is a large, casual place for good seafood and ceviche. The lunch-only **Segundo Muelle** (Conquistadores 490, tel. 01/421-1206, www.segundomuelle.com, noon–5 P.M. daily, US$8–12) successfully combines pastas with seafood and tasty ceviche. Try the ravioli stuffed with crabmeat or lasagna with shrimp and artichoke.

San Isidro's classic Peruvian restaurant, with 35 years in the business, is **José Antonio** (Bernardo Monteagudo 200, tel. 01/264-0188, www.joseantonio.com.pe, 12:30–4:30 P.M. and 7:30 P.M.–midnight daily, US$14–17). Said to have the best *lomo saltado* in town, the restaurant also offers *ají de gallina, cau cau,* and *causa* with *camarones.*

International

With a culture of ceviche, it isn't surprising

that Lima has latched on to sushi. **Osaka** (Conquistadores 999, tel. 01/222-0405, www.osakafusion.com, 12:30–4 P.M. and 7:30 P.M.–1 A.M. daily, US$9–12) is doing with Japanese food what many Peruvian restaurants have done with international cuisine: fusion. *Camote* (sweet potato) tempura and Inca rolls are dinner highlights. **Asia de Cuba** (Conquistadores 780, San Isidro, tel. 01/222-4940, www.asiadecubaperu.com, 7 P.M.–close Mon.–Sat., US$15) is a swanky sushi house with over-the-top decor. There are more than 30 types of martinis, a range of buttery sushi, and other Asian fusion cuisine.

A casual place for great Mexican and margaritas is **Como Agua Para Chocolate** (Pancho Fierro 108, tel. 01/222-0297, noon–midnight Mon.–Sat., noon–10 P.M. Sun., US$8), with brightly colored walls and friendly service. If you are in the mood for an Argentine grill, and an all-meat menu, head to **La Carreta** (Rivera Navarrete 740, tel. 01/442-2690, 11 A.M.–11 P.M. daily, US$20–30).

Fine Dining

Featured in many local cookbooks, the recipes of **Malabar** (Camino Real 101, tel. 01/440-5200, 12:30–3:30 P.M. and 7:30–11:30 P.M., US$15–20) have garnered national acclaim. The flavors are a mix of the Mediterranean (chef Pedro Miguel Schiaffino studied in Italy), Amazonia (then he lived in Iquitos), and finally classic Peruvian. The intimate restaurant, with clean white tablecloths, is the perfect fusion for a traveler who's been all over the country.

To live classic Lima's elegance, you can do nothing better than have a pisco sour on the wide open patio of **Perroquet** (Los Eucaliptos 590, tel. 01/611-9000, www.hotelcountry.com, 11 A.M.–11 P.M. daily, US$15–20), inside the Country Club Lima Hotel. Follow your sour with grilled chita fish, and finally top it off with a medley of Peruvian fruit sorbets.

With only 10 tables, the city's most intimate seafood restaurant is probably **El Kapallaq** (Petit Thouars 4844, tel. 01/444-4149, noon–5 P.M. daily, US$14–18). The owner, of Basque ancestry, throws in twists from his home country, dishing up favorites like *marmitako* (a seafood stew). But the Peruvian influence is just as strong, and classics like *arroz con conchas y langostinos* (rice with scallops and shrimp) and *chita* (Peruvian grunt fish) are also present. This classic restaurant is a lunch-only establishment. With a steel bed on its entrance patio and a dining room full of round mirrors, **Restaurante Rodrigo** (Francisco de Paula Camino 231, tel. 01/446-0985, www.restauranterodrigo.com, 1–4 P.M. and 8 P.M.–midnight, US$20–25) is Lima's chic and cosmopolitian, Basque-influenced restaurant. Here, the precursor to dinner is an appetizer sampler, each shot-glass-size, including spinach salad and pork mousse with applesauce. Dinner is calamari stuffed with rich risotto or halibut served over black rice.

MIRAFLORES

Even if you are on a limited budget, splurging on one of Miraflores's top restaurants will be a memorable experience you will not regret.

Cafés, Bakeries, and Ice Cream

One of Lima's classic cafés is surely **Haiti** (Diagonal 160, tel. 01/446-3816, 7 A.M.–2 A.M. Sun.–Thurs., 7 A.M.–3 A.M. Fri.–Sat., US$9), in operation for more than half a century on Parque Kennedy. Indoor and sidewalk tables are overflowing with Peruvians day and night. Haiti is less known for its food than its intellectual conversation, good coffee, and pisco sours. Right across the street is **La Tiendecita Blanca** (Larco 111, tel. 01/445-1412, 7 A.M.–midnight daily, US$11), an elegant Swiss-style café and deli that has been in business since 1937. Anything you eat here will be excellent. This is Miraflores's most happening business breakfast spot, and in the evenings, steamy fondues emerge from the kitchen.

The youthful, trendy **Café Zeta** (Oscar Benavides 598, tel. 01/444-5579, 7 A.M.–11:30 P.M. daily, US$6–10) is straight out of Chicago. Here you can sip mango tea while nibbling banana bread, or down a big sandwich and beer.

Ugo, the Italian owner of **La Bodega de la Trattoria** (General Borgoño 784, tel. 01/241-6899, 7:30 A.M.–2 A.M. daily, US$9–13), claims that sitting on his patio is almost like being on a European plaza. His Italian menu and strong espressos aid in the illusion, and the effect is the whiling away of a Lima afternoon. Meals are also served.

Try the *lomo saltado* sandwich at **Pasquale Hnos. Sangucheria** (Comandante Espinar 651, tel. 01/447-6390, noon–10 P.M. Mon.–Fri., 10 A.M.–1 A.M. Sat., 10 A.M.–midnight Sun., US$6). This sandwich joint makes fast food fancy and purely Peruvian, since all sandwiches are inspired by classic Peruvian plates. **San Antonio** (Vasco Núñez de Balboa 762, tel. 01/241-3001, 7 A.M.–11 P.M. daily) is a bakery/café/deli with 35 gourmet sandwiches (including smoked salmon and Italian salami), huge salads with organic lettuce, and an extensive dessert case with an out-of-this-world *tortaleta de lúcuma*. Across the street, **T'anta** (28 de Julio 888, tel. 01/447-8377, 7 A.M.–midnight Mon.–Sat., 7 A.M.–10 P.M. Sun.) is similarly gourmet, but the menu is all Peruvian.

Your dessert choices are twofold, chocolate or ice cream. Limeños are right when they say that **Quattro D** (Angamos Oeste 408, tel. 01/447-1523, 6:30 A.M.–12:30 A.M. Sun.–Fri., 6:30 A.M.–1:30 A.M. Sat.) has the best ice cream and gelato in Lima, but at **Chocolates Helena** (Chiclayo 897, tel. 01/242-8899, www.chocolateshelena.com, 10:30 A.M.–7:30 P.M. daily) the *chocotejas* and truffles are hard to resist.

Ceviche

An upscale *cebichería,* **Alfresco** (Malecón Balta 790, tel. 01/444-7962, 9 A.M.–5 P.M. daily, US$12–14) serves grilled shrimp, clams, and a special *cebiche alfresco* with three sauces. This stylish place also serves tempting desserts, such as *crocante de lúcuma* and *suspiro de Limeña,* and international wines. At a more affordable price, **Punto Azul** (San Martin 395, tel. 01/445-8078, 11 A.M.–4 P.M. Mon.–Fri., 11 A.M.–5 P.M. Sat.–Sun. US$7–9) serves a similar menu. One plate is enough for two, but arrive early because after 1:30 P.M. you'll have to wait to get a seat.

Ceviche is elegantly served in martini glasses at Gaston Acurio's **La Mar Cebichería** (La Mar 770, tel. 01/421-3365, 11 A.M.–5 P.M., US$15–20). No reservations are accepted and lines can get long, so plan for a leisurely lunch over several types of ceviche, cold beer, grilled fish, and crisp white wine.

Peruvian

One of the greatest Peruvian comfort foods is the creamy potato-based *causa,* and now, there is an entire restaurant devoted to it. **Mi Causa** (La Mar 814, tel. 01/222-6258, www.micausaperu.com, noon–5:30 P.M. daily, US$10–12) has the classic tuna and avocado offerings, but why not try a *lomo saltado* or *cauchi de camarones* (crayfish stew) *causa?*

Budget eaters flock to **Rincón Chami** (Esperanza 154, tel. 01/444-4511, 9 A.M.–9 P.M. Mon.–Sat., 9 A.M.–5 P.M. Sun., US$7) for ceviche, tamales, *brochetas,* and *lomo saltados,* dished up in a dinerlike atmosphere. Each day there is a different special of the house (Sunday, for instance, it's *chupe de camarones,* a cream-based soup with sea shrimp).

International

La Trattoria di Mambrino (Manuel Bonilla 106, tel. 01/446-1192, 1–3:30 P.M. and 8:30–11:30 P.M. Mon.–Sat., 1–3:30 P.M. Sun., US$10–12) is owned by a Roman and may be Peru's best Italian restaurant. This cozy place serves authentic Italian dishes like gnocchi with pesto genovese, risotto with wild mushrooms, panfried shrimp with wine sauce, and porcini mushroom pizza.

For Middle Eastern food, stop in at **Tarboush** (Diagonal 358, tel. 01/242-6994, 9 A.M.–midnight Mon.–Thurs., 9 A.M.–1 A.M. Fri.–Sat., 10 A.M.–11 P.M. Sun., US$5–6), with sidewalk tables across from Parque Kennedy. Lamb kebabs, Greek salads, tabouli, and falafel are prepared fresh for incredibly cheap prices. Don't miss the *lúcuma* juice.

Located at Larcomar mall, **Makoto** (Malecón de la Reserva 610, tel. 01/444-5030, www.larcomar.com, 11 A.M.–7 P.M. Mon.–Sat., 11 A.M.–3 P.M. Sun., US$20) is an excellent,

though touristy, sushi restaurant with high prices. **Edo Sushi Bar** (Berlin 601, tel. 01/243-2448, www.edosushibar.com, 12:30–3:30 P.M. and 7–11 P.M. Mon.–Sat., US$10) is a cool, quiet restaurant for authentic sushi.

Fine Dining

Our vote for best restaurant in Peru is **Astrid y Gastón** (Cantuarias 175, tel. 01/444-1496, 1–3 P.M. and 7:30–11:30 P.M. Mon.–Sat., US$35–40). This adventurous gourmet restaurant, set in an elegant republican-style home, is the labor of love of a Peruvian-German couple who met at the Cordon Bleu in Paris. The evening begins with creative pisco drinks such as the *aguaymanto* sour, made with *pisco puro* and the tangy juice of *aguaymanto* fruit. Then, as diners watch through a glass wall, chefs concoct never-before-sampled entrées such as kid goat basted in *algarroba* honey and marinated in *chicha de jora,* or river prawns served with red curry, coconut milk, and jasmine rice. Save room; the desserts are the best part: *blanco mousse* with a sauce of *sauco* and blackberries.

You will not regret the cab ride to **Pescados Capitales** (La Mar 1337, tel. 01/421-8808, 12:30–5 P.M. Tues.–Sun., US$10), a witty play on words (*pescados* means fish but rhymes with *pecados,* or sins) that makes sense when you see the menu. Each dish is named for a virtue or sin; Diligence will bring you a ceviche of tuna and *conchas negras,* while Patience will bring you a ceviche of shrimps with curry and mango chutney.

The elegant **Huaca Pucllana** (General Borgoño block 8, tel. 01/445-4042, noon–4 P.M. and 7 P.M.–midnight daily, US$10–22) has a magical feel when the ruins of the same name, only six meters away, are lit up at night. Guests sit at linen-covered tables on an open-air patio next to the ruins and enjoy dishes such as grilled portobello mushroom salad with goat cheese, rabbit stewed in a red wine, mushroom sauce over polenta, and grilled lamb chops.

If you're in the mood for Mediterranean, head to **La Gloria** (Atahualpa 201, tel. 01/446-6504, www.lagloriarestaurant.com, 1–4 P.M.

and 8 P.M.–midnight Mon.–Sat., US$29). Especially good are the *carpaccio de pescado* with ginger and the seared tuna steaks.

Two restaurants are locked in battle for Lima's best place for *comida criolla*. **Brujas de Cachiche** (Bolognesi 460, tel. 01/446-6536, www.brujasdecachiche.com, noon–midnight Mon.–Sat., noon–4:30 P.M. Sun., US$25) has an extraordinary buffet every day of the week, except Sunday, that includes a tour de force of centuries of indigenous Peruvian cooking. **El Señorio de Sulco** (Malecón Cisneros 1470, tel. 01/441-0389, www.senoriodesulco.com, noon–midnight Mon.–Sat., noon–5 P.M. Sun., US$10–16) also has an extravagant daily lunch buffet and a range of seafood plates. Try the *chupe de camarones,* a cream-based soup full of sea shrimp, yellow potatoes, and *ají* pepper.

We think Lima's time-honored seaside gourmet restaurant, Rosa Naútica, is a bit faded. But a good contender, **Costanera 700** (El Ejército 421, tel. 01/421-4635, noon–5 P.M. and 7–11 P.M. Mon.–Sat., noon–5 P.M. Sun., US$30), is gaining ground and has been repeatedly voted one of the best restaurants in Lima. This is a good place to come for an elegant array of both Peruvian and international cuisine.

Chifa

Central Lima's time-honored *chifa* restaurant **Wa Lok** (Angamos Oeste 700, tel. 01/447-1314, noon–11:30 P.M. Mon.–Sat., noon–11 P.M. Sun., US$15–20) now has a Miraflores location. You'll have to ignore the charmless first-floor casino before you can settle down into your fish with corn sauce or steaming stir-fry.

Vegetarian

Miraflores's best vegetarian restaurant is **Govinda** (Schell 634, tel. 01/444-2871, 10:30 A.M.–8 P.M. Mon.–Sat., 11 A.M.–4:30 P.M. Sun., US$4). The creative dishes of this Hare Krishna–operated restaurant include pad thai, Asian tofu salad, and *lomo saltado* with soy meat.

When you walk through a health food store to get to the restaurant, you know lunch will be balanced and nutritious. **Madre Natura**

(Chiclayo 815, tel. 01/445-2522, 8 A.M.–9 P.M. Mon.–Sat., US$6) is all that, and well priced. Sit down for a soy-based hamburger, and leave with wheat bread in hand.

Markets

Plaza Vea (Arequipa 4651, 9 A.M.–10 P.M. daily), **Metro** (Schell 250, 9 A.M.–11 P.M. daily), and the upscale **Vivanda** (Benavides 495, 24 hours) have large selections of international and domestic foods.

BARRANCO AND THE SOUTH

Slow-paced Barranco has a number of romantic eateries and cafés, and on the weekends, outdoor food stalls fill a walkway near the central plaza.

Cafés, Bakeries, and Ice Cream

For an affordable lunch *menú,* head to **Iskay Cafeteria & Artensía** (Pedro de Osma 106, tel. 01/247-2102, 9 A.M.–midnight daily, US$6–8). Pastas, sandwiches, and *piqueos* are the specialties. Stop by **Café Cultural Restaurante** (San Martín 15-A, tel. 01/247-5131, 9 A.M.–2 A.M., US$4–8), in a 1920s English train car, for a drink, but skip the food. The best café is on the open-air patio of **Dédalo,** the artisan shop.

Ceviche

CantaRana (Génova 101, tel. 01/247-7274, 9 A.M.–11 P.M. Tues.–Sat., 11 A.M.–6 P.M. Sun., US$8–11), a no-frills lunch place with loads of history, serves up great *cebiche* and a range of seafood. The unassuming **Costa Sur** (Chorrillos 180, tel. 01/252-0150, 11:30 A.M.–5 P.M. Tues.–Sun., US$8–10), in Chorrillos, has fried shrimp and *conchas a la parmesana* worth a taxi ride.

Peruvian

With bow tie–clad waiters and an old piano, **Las Mesitas** (Grau 341, tel. 01/477-4199, noon–1 A.M. daily, US$5–7) has an old-timey feel. For those on a budget, this is a great place to sample Peruvian food, including *humitas,* tamales, *sopa criolla, ocopa arequipeña,* and *lomo saltado.*

Lunch buffets are popular in Lima, and

Barranco seems to have an especially high per capita number of restaurants serving up just that. In order of preference, we recommend: **Puro Perú** (República de Panamá 258, tel. 01/477-0111, 12:30–5 P.M. daily, US$15) and the oceanside **Rustica** (Playa Barranco, tel. 01/9403-4679, 12:30 P.M.–midnight daily, US$15).

Mi Perú (Av. Lima 861, Plaza Butters, tel. 01/247-7682, noon–5:30 P.M. daily, US$8–10) is what you call in Peru a *huarique*, a hole-in-the-wall with good food. In this case it's all about the *concentrado de cangrejo* (crab soup), the best you will try in all Peru. *Cebiches* are good here, too, but go for the soup. It's worth every penny.

For a steak and red wine fix, **Parrilladas El Hornero** (Malecón Grau 983, tel. 01/251-8109, noon–midnight Mon.–Sat., noon–6 P.M. Sun., US$8–10), in Chorrillos, is a must. The second-floor tables have impressive ocean views, and the grilled provolone and Argentine baby beef will do for your palate what it won't do for your cholesterol.

Fine Dining

Amor Amar (Jirón Garcia y García 175, tel. 01/651-1111, US$10–25) is the newest and smartest restaurant in town, and it happens to be in Barranco. Luis Alberto Sacilotto, the renowned chef of La Gloria, and the owners of Pescados Capitales decided to open this new culinary (ad)venture. The food is incredibly good, having on the menu *cebiches, tiraditos,* and grilled octopus, among other seafood specialties. Other options include risottos, duck, lamb, and beef. Cocktails are well done and the varied wine list is pretty impressive.

Pizza

The best pizzas are at the new **Antica Trattoria** (San Martín 201, tel. 01/247-3443, 12:30 P.M.–midnight daily, US$7–10), a charming Italian eatery with stucco walls, exposed beams, and rustic furniture. The lasagna here is excellent, as is the array of homemade pastas.

Markets

The large modern supermarket **Metro** (Grau 513, 9 A.M.–10:30 P.M. daily) is within walking distance from all Barranco hotels.

Information and Services

TOURIST INFORMATION

Free maps and tourist information are available at **Iperú** (Jorge Chávez Airport, main hall, tel. 01/574-8000, www.peru.info, 24 hours daily). There are other branches in San Isidro (Jorge Basadre 610, tel. 01/421-1627, 8:30 A.M.–6 P.M. Mon.–Fri.) and Miraflores (Larcomar, tel. 01/445-9400, noon–8 P.M. daily).

The best source of travel information in Peru, along with maps, advice, trip reports, restaurant and hotel discounts, and all-around friendly people, is the amazing, Miraflores-based **South American Explorers Club** (Piura 135, Miraflores, tel. 01/445-3306, www.saexplorers.org, 9:30 A.M.–5 P.M. Mon.–Fri., 9:30 A.M.–1 P.M. Sat.).

In Barranco, **Intej** (San Martín 240, tel. 01/247-3230, www.intej.org, 9:30 A.M.–12:45 P.M. daily) is the Lima base for all student travel organizations. Student travel cards can be acquired here with a letter on the appropriate stationery, and student flights can be changed.

MAPS

The easiest place to buy maps is in **Miraflores** at the **South American Explorers Club,** which has good maps of Lima, the Huaraz area, and Peru in general. It also sells the more popular of Peru's military topographic maps.

If you are planning on driving or biking through Peru, excellent driving maps and information are contained in *Inca Guide to Peru* (Peisa, 2002), which is available in most bookshops. Another recommended series is published by Lima 2000 and also available in bookshops.

© RENÉE DEL GAUDIO AND ROSS WEHNER

Giant teddy bears and other oddities are for sale in the street market behind Lima's main post office.

For hard-to-find topo maps, head to **Surquillo** and the **Instituto Geográfico Nacional** (Aramburu 1180, tel. 01/475-3085, www.ignperu.gob.pe, 8 A.M.–6 P.M. Mon.–Fri.), which also sells digital, geological, and departmental maps.

POLICE AND FIRE

Through **Iperú's** 24-hour stand (tel. 01/574-8000) in the main hall of the airport, you can report tourist-related crimes. The headquarters of the national police are in **Lince** (Pezet y Miel 1894, tel. 01/373-2423, www.pnp.gob.pe), and the tourist police have an office in **Magdalena** (Moore 268, tel. 01/460-0849, dipolture@hotmail.com). Dialing 105 also reaches police from a private phone, or dial 116 for the **fire department.**

IMMIGRATIONS OFFICE

Lima's **Migraciones** (immigrations office) is near the center (España 734, Breña, tel. 01/330-4144, 8 A.M.–1 P.M. Mon.–Fri.). Arrive early and with US$20 if you want to receive a new visa the same day.

HEALTH CARE

Lima has Peru's best hospitals, and it is easy, and quite inexpensive, to get parasite tests and yellow fever or tetanus shots.

Perhaps the easiest option, if you need a doctor, is to call **Doctor Más** (tel. 01/444-9377), a company that, for US$40, will send an English-speaking doctor to your hotel to check on you and write a prescription. Doctor Más physicians can also be reached directly on their cell phones. Try **Dr. Ana del Aguila** (tel. 01/9818-2561) or **Dr. Jorge Garmendia** (tel. 01/9818-2554). You can even pay with a credit card if you notify them while setting up the visit.

If you prefer a clinic, all of the places listed have English-speaking doctors. In central Lima, the **Clínica International** (Washington 1471, 8 A.M.–8 P.M. Mon.–Fri., 8 A.M.–2 P.M. Sat.) will see walk-in patients for about US$30. Doctor's visits at both places cost around US$30.

The best (and most expensive) medical care in Peru is in **San Isidro** at the **Clínica Anglo-**

Americana (Alfredo Salazar, block 3 s/n, tel. 01/712-3000, www.clinangloamericana.com. pe, 8 A.M.–8 P.M. Mon.–Fri., 9 A.M.–noon Sat.), which charges US$60 for a doctor's visit.

In **Miraflores,** a high-quality option is **Clínica Good Hope** (Malecón Balta 956, tel. 01/241-3256, www.goodhope.org.pe, 9 A.M.–midnight), which charges about US$40 for a doctor's visit. For lab testing and shots, **Suiza Lab** (Angamos Oeste 300, tel. 01/612-6666, www.suizalab.com.pe, 9 A.M.–midnight) is very professional, clean, and reasonably priced. With dental problems, call **Dr. Flavio Larrain** (Pasaje Sucre 154, tel. 01/445 2586, 8 A.M.–7 P.M. Mon.–Fri.), who charges US$50 for a checkup and cleaning.

Pharmacies

Most pharmacies are willing to deliver to your hotel. Near central Lima, the **Metro supermarket** in Breña (corner of Venezuela and Alfonso Ugarte) has a good pharmacy. In San Isidro, try **Deza** (Conquistadores 1144, San Isidro, tel. 01/442-9196, 24 hours). In Miraflores, try **InkaFarma** (tel. 01/314-2020, www.inkafarma.com.pe, delivery service), **Farmacias 24 Horas** (tel. 01/444-0568), **Botica Fasa** (Larco 135, www.boticasfasa. com.pe), **Superfarma** (Benavides 2849, tel. 01/222-1575, or Armendariz 215, tel. 01/440-9000).

BANKS AND MONEY EXCHANGE

For those just arriving in Peru, there are two exchange houses inside the Lima airport that change travelers checks for a 2.5 percent commission. In general, the best place to cash travelers checks is at any Banco de Crédito, which charges the lowest commission—1.8 percent. ATMs are now ubiquitous across Lima (and most of Peru). Almost all work with Visa, MasterCard, and Cirrus, and Interbank's Global Net and Banco de Crédito even handle American Express. Take care when getting money at night; it's a good idea to have a taxi waiting.

Money-change houses (*casas de cambio*) offer slightly better rates than banks and are mercifully free of the hour-long lines that snake inside most banks. There are a few change houses on Larco in Miraflores and on Ocoña in central Lima. Be careful changing money with people on the street, even if they do have the requisite badge and bright-yellow vest. Safe places for money-changing on the street are Parque Kennedy or Pardo and Comandante Espinar in Miraflores.

Here is an alphabetical listing of banks and money changers, by neighborhood. Banks are generally open 9 A.M.–6 P.M. Monday–Friday and 9 A.M. 12:30 P.M. Saturday. All banks are closed on Sunday.

In central Lima, there's **Banco Continental** (Abancay 260-262, tel. 01/427-4623), **Banco de Crédito** (Washington 1600, tel. 01/433-2785), **Interbank** (Jr. de la Unión tel. 01/536-544), **Scotiabank** (Camaná 623-627, tel. 01/211-6000), and **Western Union** (Carabaya 693, tel. 01/427-9845), for wiring money. A recommended change house is **Lac Dolar** (Camaná 779, tel. 01/428-8127).

San Isidro, Lima's financial district, has a **Banco Continental** (Camino Real 355, tel. 01/440-4553), **Banco de Crédito** (Jorge Basadre 301, tel. 01/440-7366), an **Interbank** (Jorge Basadre 391-395), **Scotiabank** (Carnaval y Moreyra 282, tel. 01/222-6567), and **Western Union** (Petit Thouars 3595, tel. 01/422-0014).

Miraflores's banks are generally clustered around the Parque Kennedy: **American Express** (Santa Cruz 621, Miraflores, tel. 01/221-8204, 9 A.M.–5:30 P.M. Mon.–Fri., 9 A.M.–1 P.M. Sat.), which will replace its traveler checks; **Banco Continental** (Pardo 791-795, tel. 01/241-5853); **Banco de Crédito** (Av. Larco 1085 tel. 01/447-1690); **Interbank** (Larco 690); **Scotiabank** (Av. Diagonal 176, tel. 01/242-3797); and a **Western Union** (Larco 826, tel. 01/241-1220). **Lac Dolar** (La Paz 211, tel. 01/242-4069) will change travelers checks for a 2 percent commission and is open 9:30 A.M.–6 P.M. Monday–Saturday.

Even quiet Barranco has a selection of financial institutions: **Banco Continental** (Grau

414, tel. 01/477-0280); **Banco de Crédito** (José M. Eguren 599, Ex-Grau), tel. 01/477-0101); **Interbank** (Grau 300); **Scotiabank** (Grau 422, tel. 01/477-0604); and **Western Union** (Grau 422, tel. 01/477-4337).

COMMUNICATIONS

The main **post office** (www.serpost.com.pe) is on the corner of **central Lima's** Plaza Mayor (Pasaje Piura, s/n, 8 A.M.–8 P.M. Mon.–Sat., 8 A.M.–3 P.M. Sun.). The **Miraflores** branch (Petit Thouars 5201, tel. 01/511-5018, 8 A.M.–8:45 P.M. Mon.–Sat., 8:45 A.M.–2 P.M. Sun.) has slightly different hours. There is also **FedEx** (Pasaje Olaya 260, Surco, tel. 01/242-2280) and **DHL** (Los Castaños 225, San Isidro, tel. 01/422-5232).

High-speed Internet is ubiquitous in Lima. In **central Lima,** try **Internet** (Pasaje Santa Rosa 165, Center, 7:30 A.M.–9 P.M. daily, US$0.75/hr). Recommended places in **Miraflores** are **@lf.net** (Manuel Bonilla 126, 9 A.M.–10 P.M. Mon.–Fri., 11 A.M.–8 P.M. Sat.–Sun., US$0.50/hour), **Refugio Internet** (Larco 1185, tel. 01/242-5910, 8:30 A.M.–11 P.M. Mon.–Fri., 9:30 A.M.–11 P.M. Sat., 10:30 A.M.–11 P.M. Sun., US$0.75/hour), and the helpful and cheap **Via Planet** (Diez Canseco 339, 9 A.M.–midnight daily, US$0.30/hour). These places do Internet calls as well.

For local calls or national calls, buy a 147 card and dial away from Telefónica booths on nearly every corner.

For international calls, put away those phone cards, because new generation cable and satellite shops offer crystal-clear communication for as low as US$0.15 per minute to the United States. **Call Center USA** (Junín 410, four blocks toward Vía Expresa from Arequipa and near the Home Peru hostel, 9 A.M.–midnight daily) offers cable calls to the United States (US$0.15/min), Europe (US$0.20/min.), or Asia (US$0.25/min.). This place also has high-speed Internet.

NEWSPAPERS

Lima's largest newspaper is **El Comercio** (www.elcomercioperu.com.pe), but we personally prefer the tabloid-format **La República** (www.larepublica.com.pe) for its daily **Mirko Lauer** political column and a more straightforward approach to news. Lima's best magazine for news, humor, and cultural information is, hands down, **Caretas. Etiqueta Negra** (www.etiquetanegra.com.pe) is a literary/social commentary magazine, and **Bocón** (www.elbocon.com.pe) is the soccer paper.

LANGUAGE SCHOOLS

There are many Spanish schools in Lima, though getting away from all the English speakers is a challenge. **San Isidro** language schools include **Instituto de Idiomas** (Camino Real 1037, tel. 01/442-8761, www.pucp.edu.pe, 11 A.M.–1 P.M. daily), which charges US$105 for 36 hours of lessons. **Asociación Cultural Peruano-Británico** (Arequipa 3495, tel. 01/221-7550, www.britanico.edu.pe) charges US$66 for 36 hours of lessons.

In **Miraflores, Instituto Cultural Peruano-Norteamericano** (Angamos Oeste 160, Miraflores, tel. 01/241-1940, www.icpna.edu.pe) charges US$54 for 40 hours of lessons plus US$82 in materials.

For a well-rounded Spanish school, try **El Sol** (Grimaldo de Solar 469, Miraflores, tel. 01/242-7763, www.idiomasperu.com), which has a Survival Spanish program for travelers that includes cooking and dancing classes, city walks, volunteer opportunities, conversation partners, and family homestays. El Sol charges US$15 per hour for small group lessons or US$110 for 10 hours of semi-intensive classes. The one-week program for beginners is US$50.

For one-on-one lessons, some recommended private tutors are **Lourdes Galvez** (tel. 01/435-3910, US$5/hour), **Llorgelina Savastaizagal** (tel. 01/275-6460, US$5/hour), and **Alex Boris** (tel. 01/423-0697, US$5/hour).

FILM AND CAMERAS

Lima's best developing and camera repair shop is **Taller de Fotografía Profesional** (Benavides 1171, tel. 01/241-1015). Other top-quality developing with one-day service is available from

Laboratorio Color Profesional (Benavides 1171, tel. 01/214-8430, 9 A.M.–7 P.M. Mon.–Fri., 9:30 A.M.–1 P.M. Sat.). A cheaper option is **Kodak Express** (9 A.M.–9 P.M. Mon.–Sat.), with offices in Miraflores (Larco 1005), San Isidro (Las Begonias), and central Lima (Unión 790, Centro). For camera repairs in the center, try **Reparación** (Cusco 592, central Lima, 4th Fl., tel. 01/426-7920, 10 A.M.–2 P.M. Mon.–Fri.). For digital camera technical glitches contact **Jorge Li Pun** (General Silva 496, Miraflores, tel. 01/447-7302, 10:30 A.M.–8 P.M. Mon.–Fri.).

LAUNDRY

In **Breña** try **Lavandería KIO** (España 481, tel. 01/332-9035, 7 A.M.–8 P.M. daily, US$1/kg). There's also a branch in **Pueblo Libre** (La Mar 1953, 2nd Fl., tel. 01/428-2776, delivery).

In **San Isidro, Lava Center** (Victor Maurtua 140, San Isidro, tel. 01/440-3600, 9:30 A.M.–8 P.M. Mon.–Fri., 9:30 A.M.–6 P.M. Sat., US$1/kg) is reliable.

Recommended places in **Miraflores** are **Servirap** (Schell 601, Miraflores, tel. 01/241-0759, 8 A.M.–10 P.M. Mon.–Sat., 10 A.M.–6 P.M. Sun., US$2.50/kg), which offers drop-off and self-service, and **Lavandería Cool Wash** (Diez Canseco 347, tel. 01/242-3882, 8:30 A.M.–7:30 P.M. Mon.–Sat.).

LUGGAGE STORAGE

Besides your hotel, you can also store bags at the airport for US$6 per day. **South American Explorers Club** members can store luggage at the clubhouse (Piura 135, Miraflores) free of charge.

Getting There and Around

AIR

Lima's international airport is **Jorge Chávez** (tel. 01/595-0606, www.lap.com.pe), 16 kilometers west of the city center at Callao.

The leading domestic airline, with international flights as well, is **LAN** (Pardo 513, Miraflores, tel. 01/213-8200, www.lan.com). It flies to all major Peruvian airports, including Trujillo, Chiclayo, Tumbes, Arequipa, Cusco, Puerto Maldonado, and Juliaca.

Useful for specific domestic routes are **Star Perú** (Pardo 269, Miraflores, tel. 01/705-9000, www.starperu.com.pe) for Trujillo, Chiclayo, Iquitos, Yurimaguas, and Tarapoto; **Aerocondor** (Juan de Aroma 781, San Isidro, tel. 01/614-6014, www.aerocondor.com.pe) for Cajamarca, Ayacucho, Talara, and Piura; **LC Busre** (Los Tulipanes 218, Lince, tel. 01/619-1313, www.lcbusre.com.pe) for Huaraz, Huánuco, and Pucallpa; and **TACA** (Comandante Espinar 331, tel. 01/511-8222, www.taca.com) for Cusco.

All of the international airlines that fly into Peru also have offices in Lima, including **Aerolíneas Argentinas** (Carnaval y Moreyra 370, San Isidro, tel. 01/513-6565, www.aerolineas.com.ar), **AeroMexico** (Pardo y Aliaga 699, of. 501, San Isidro, tel. 01/705-1111, www.aeromexico.com), **American Airlines** (Las Begonias 471, San Isidro, tel. 01/211-7000, www.aa.com.pe), **Avianca** (José Pardo 14, Miraflores, tel. 01/445-9902, www.avianca.com), **Continental Airlines** (Victor Andrés Belaúnde 147, of. 101, San Isidro, tel. 01/221-4340, www.continental.com), **Copa Airlines** (Carnaval y Moreyra and Los Halcones, San Isidro, tel. 01/610-0808, www.copaair.com), **Delta Air Lines** (Victor Andrés Belaúnde 147, of. 701, San Isidro, tel. 01/211-9211, www.delta.com), **KLM** (Alvarez Calderon 185, of. 601, San Isidro, tel. 01/213-0200, www.klm.com), **Lloyd Aero Boliviano** (José Pardo 231, Miraflores, tel. 01/241-5513, www.labairlines.com.bo), and **Taca Peru** (Comandante Espinar 331, Miraflores, tel. 01/231-7000, www.taca.com).

BUS

Highways in Peru have improved immensely over the last decade, making in-country bus travel not only cheap but efficient. From Lima,

© PROMPERU

Lima's main highway, the Via Expresa, at night

buses head to every major city in Peru except water-locked Iquitos. The South American Explorers Club has an excellent Lima folder with a detailed rundown of bus companies and the schedules. Unfortunately, there is no main bus station in Lima. Instead, companies have their own terminals in the center and sometimes also on Javier Prado or Paseo de la República near San Isidro. All of these neighborhoods are rough, so take a taxi to and from the terminal and keep a hand on all your belongings.

The two classic and reputable bus companies in Lima are Cruz del Sur and Ormeño. Movil Tours and the new Oltursa, however, both get consistently strong reviews. **Cruz del Sur** has a terminal in the center (Quilca 531, tel. 01/451-5125) and near San Isidro (corner of Javier Prado Este 1100, tel. 01/225-5748). Though it does not go as many places as Ormeño, Cruz del Sur's Cruzero is the most comprehensive bus service in Peru. Best of all, tickets can be bought instantly online, from any agency in Lima, or at the TeleTicket counters at Wong and Metro supermarkets (in Miraflores there

is a Wong at Óvalo Gutierrez and a Metro at Schell 250, near Parque Kennedy). Spanish speakers can even call the Cruz del Sur call center (tel. 01/311-5050, have passport number ready) and have their tickets delivered free of charge. Payment is in cash upon receipt of tickets. Buses leave first from the central Lima terminal and pick up passengers a half hour later at the Javier Prado terminal. For complete route information, see the website www.cruzdelsur.com.pe.

Ormeño also has a terminal in the center (Carlos Zavala 177, tel. 01/427-5679, www.grupo-ormeno.com) and an international terminal near San Isidro (Javier Prado Este 1059, La Victoria, tel. 01/472-1710). Ormeño has better coverage and is slightly cheaper than Cruz del Sur. To buy an Ormeño ticket, visit a terminal, go through an agency (the agency will get the tickets a few hours later), or call the Spanish-only call center (tel. 01/472-5000). Again, have passport number when calling and cash in hand when the ticket is delivered.

The highly recommended **Movil Tours** (Paseo de la República 749, La Victoria, tel.

LIMA BUS SCHEDULE

The following is a thumbnail of bus trip duration and prices to/from Lima with a range from economical to luxury service. At the bottom end, buses stop frequently, are crowded, and lack bathrooms. The top-end buses are decked out with reclining semibeds, clean bathrooms, onboard food and beverage service, video, and a second story with great views. Prices increase 50 percent around holidays, including Christmas, Easter, and the July 28 Fiestas Patrias weekend.

CITY	PRICE	TIME
Arequipa	US$20-48	13-15 hours
Ayacucho	US$20-30	8-9 hours
Cajamarca	US$25-48	14 hours
Chachapoyas	US$16-35	25 hours
Chanchamayo	US$19-27	8 hours
Chiclayo	US$19-36	10 hours
Cusco	US$26-37	52 hours
Huancayo	US$17-26	7 hours
Huaraz	US$20-26	8 hours
Máncora	US$28-57	16-17 hours
Nasca	US$20-31	8 hours
Pisco	US$18-28	4 hours
Piura	US$25-38	14-15 hours
Puno	US$34-60	21-24 hours
Tacna	US$37-50	18-20 hours
(Chile border)		
Trujillo	US$16-34	8 hours
Tumbes	US$30-57	18 hours
(Ecuador border)		

recommended for its service (some claim that it's better than Cruz del Sur), and advance reservations can be made by telephone or online.

Phone reservations do not work well at the other companies. Your best bet is to buy tickets at the terminal.

Expreso Wari (Montevideo 809, central Lima, tel. 01/330-3518) goes to Nasca, Ayacucho, and Cusco.

Empresa Molina (Nicolas Arriola and San Luis, central Lima, tel. 01/342-2137) goes to Huancayo, Ayacucho, and Cusco.

Enlaces (Javier Prado Este 1093, La Victoria, tel. 01/265-9041) runs between Lima and Arequipa.

Flores has the best coverage of the small bus companies, lower prices, and a terminal in both central Lima (Montevideo 523) and near San Isidro (Paseo de la República 627, La Victoria). It has cheap buses for Arequipa, Cajamarca, Chiclayo, Máncora, Nasca, Piura, Puno, Tacna, Trujillo, and Tumbes. With questions, call 01/332-1212 or enter the company's website at www.floreshnos.com.

Mariscal Cáceres has offices both in central Lima (Carlos Zavala 211, tel. 01/427-2844) and near San Isidro (28 de Julio 2195, La Victoria, tel. 01/225-2532) and heads primarily to Huancayo.

Soyuz (Carlos Zavala 217, tel. 01/266-1515, www.soyuz.com.pe) has good frequency on the south coast.

Companies whose travelers report frequent delays, breakdowns, or other problems include **Tepsa** and **Civa**.

Recommended international companies are Caracol, Ormeño, and El Rápido.

Caracol (Brasil 425, Jesus María, tel. 01/431-1400, www.perucaracol.com) receives the best reviews and covers the entire continent. It partners with Cruz del Sur so you can buy tickets from either company's terminals. Among other places, Caracol travels to Santiago, Chile; Santa Cruz and La Paz, Bolivia; Asunción, Paraguay; Córdoba and Buenos Aires, Argentina; Montevideo, Uruguay; São Paulo and Rio de Janeiro, Brazil; and Quito and Guayaquil, Ecuador.

01/332-9000, www.moviltours.com.pe) has a station near San Isidro and runs mainly to the northern cities, including Huaraz, Chachapoyas, and Chiclayo, and is about the same price as Ormeño. Phone reservations are accepted for payment at terminal.

The local favorite, **Oltursa** (Av. Aramburu 1160, Surquillo, tel. 01/225-4499, www.oltursa.com.pe), runs primarily a coastal route, both north and south of Lima. The destinations of Arequipa and Chiclayo are the exceptions to that rule. The company comes highly

Ormeño (Javier Prado Este 1059, tel. 01/472-1710) no longer travels to Brazil but does go to Bogatá, Colombia; Santiago, Chile; Buenos Aires, Argentina; and Guayaquil, Ecuador.

El Rápido (Rivera Navarrete 2650, Lince, tel. 01/425-1066) has cheaper fares to Santiago, Chile; and Buenos Aires, Argentina.

TRAIN

Between May and October, a passenger train still departs on Fridays from Lima's antique Desamparados train station downtown. After climbing the steep valley above Lima it crests the Andes at 4,751 meters (nearly 15,700 feet!) and continues to Huancayo. Trains return from Huancayo to Lima on Sunday evening, making for an interesting weekend outing.

Sunday excursion trains also leave the station for San Bartolomé, a country hamlet 1.5 hours by train outside Lima that is often sunny when the city is fogged in. These trains leave at 6 A.M. and return at 6 P.M. For tickets and exact departure information, contact the **Desamparados train station** (Ancash 201, tel. 01/361-2828, ext. 222).

LOCAL TRANSPORTATION
Taxi

If you want to make a spare buck in Lima, buy a taxi sticker from the market for US$0.50, plop it on your windshield, and start picking up passengers. Understandably, the vast majority of taxis in Lima are unofficial and unregulated, and assaults on passengers picked up at the airport occur occasionally.

The best way to take a taxi is to call a registered company and pay an additional 30–50 percent. Recommended taxi companies include **Taxi Lima** (tel. 01/213-5050, daily 24 hours), **Taxi Miraflores** (tel. 01/446-4336, daily 24 hours), and **Taxi Móvil** (tel. 01/422-6890, San Isidro, daily 24 hours).

If you feel comfortable, and have a smidgen of Spanish, stand on the street until a safe-looking, registered taxi passes by. These should be painted yellow and have the taxi sign on the hood of the car and a registration sticker on the windshield. Older taxi drivers tend to be safer than young ones. Of course, avoid old cars with tinted windows and broken door handles. Bargain before you get in a taxi or you will get fleeced. Fares from the airport to Miraflores should be US$15–20, airport–center about US$15, Miraflores–center about US$6, and Miraflores–Barranco about US$4. Prices go up during rush hour and at night. Taxis can also be rented by the hour for US$12 (registered taxi) or US$8 (street taxi).

Bus and *Colectivo*

Buses and *colectivos,* or minibuses, are an interesting, economical way to travel around Lima. Bus fares are US$0.50 on weekdays and a fraction more on Sundays. *Colectivos* cost US$0.70 on weekdays and US$0.80 on Sundays. You can tell where buses and *combis* are going by the sticker on the front windshield (not by what's painted on the side). There are also slightly more expensive *colectivo* cars, which can take up to five passengers and are a bit faster than the van-style *colectivos,* which in turn are faster than buses. To get off a bus or *colectivo* simply say *"baja"* ("getting off") or *"esquina"* ("at the corner"). Have your change ready, as money is collected right before you get off.

To reach Miraflores from the center, head to Garcilaso de la Vega (formerly Wilson) and take one of the buses or *colectivos* marked Miraflores or Todo Arequipa, which go all the way to Parque Kennedy. To reach Barranco, take a bus marked Barranco/Chorrillos from the same place. Or head to Miraflores and change buses there.

From Miraflores, most buses and *colectivos* can be taken from Larco along Parque Kennedy. To reach central Lima, take the bus marked Tacna/Wilson and ask to be dropped off at the central street of Ica or Callao. To reach Barranco, take the bus marked Barranco/Chorrillos, and the airport is Faucett/Aeropuerto. However, buses for the airport aren't very reliable and at times only come within five blocks of the airport. Take a taxi and keep your luggage safe.

Car Rental

The major rental car agencies are **Hertz**

(Salaverry 2599, San Isidro, tel. 01/421-0282, airport tel. 01/517-2402, www.hertz.com.pe, 24 hours), **Budget** (Larco 998, Miraflores, tel. 01/444-4546, airport tel. 01/517-1880, www. budgetperu.com), and **Avis** (Grimaldo del Solar 236, Miraflores, tel. 01/446-3156, www. avisperu.com). There are many more options under *Automóviles-alquiler* in the yellow pages.

Private Car

Private drivers can also be hired for the hour, day, or for a trip like the Nasca Lines. Many travelers who are only in Lima for a single day would greatly benefit from a driver who recommends museums and restaurants and then drops them off at the airport in the evening. A highly recommended driver is **José Salinas Casanova** (tel. 01/9329-2614, casanovacab@hotmail.com, US$7/hr) based out of the Hotel Antigua Miraflores. **Miguel Vásquez Díaz** (Carlos Izaguirre 1353, central Lima, tel. 01/9809-2321, sumisein@latinmail. com) and English-speaking **Mónica Velasquez** (tel. 01/9943-0796 or 01/224-8608, www. monicatourism.da.ru) are also recommended. **Fidel Loayza Paredes** (tel. 01/533-1609, armandoloayza280671@hotmail.com) does not speak English but is trustworthy.

Southern Beaches

We notice with some dismay that many guidebooks give poor write-ups about the beaches just south of Lima. The general thought is that they are dirty, crowded, treacherous, and, in general, not worth visiting. Though it is true that the white sands and subtropical climate of Peru's north beaches are more alluring, they are also a 20-hour bus ride to the north of Lima. If you are in Lima and in need of a beach fix, head south for a half hour to Punta Hermosa or San Bartolo. You will find sandy beaches, world-class surfing waves, protected beaches for safe swimming, rocking nightlife, a few good hostels, and lots of *cebicherías*. The only time to visit these beaches is during the summer months from mid-December to the end of April—they are cloudy during the rest of the year. Make reservations well in advance, especially January–mid-March, when surfers from around the world flock here along with Peruvian students on summer break. The best time to go is Sunday–Thursday nights, when beaches are empty and hotel prices are often 30 percent lower than those listed.

There are other options besides Punta Hermosa and San Bartolo—check out the *Guia Inca de las Playas,* for sale at Lima bookstores, for more details. **Santa María,** at Km 48 of the Panamericana, is an upscale beach with a control point that admits only residents and respectable-looking day-trippers. If you want a fancier, clean, but fairly snobby beach experience, this is your place, though there are few or no lodging options here. **Pucusana** is a picturesque fishing town at Km 58 of the Panamericana. **Puerto Viejo,** at Km 72 of the Panamericana, is a long beach good for beginning surfers—including a left point break that ranges 1–2 meters. **Leon Dormido** (Sleeping Lion) at Km 80 has a calm beach that is often crowded. The best parties, however, are at **Asia,** Km 97, which becomes an explosion of discos, condos, private clubs, and even car dealerships in the summer. Teenagers here for the parties pack the beach and the discos at night. Near Asia's beaches, and close to shore, there are several islands with great sea kayaking and possibilities to see Humboldt penguins and sea lions. Finally, **Cerro Azul** at Km 128 is a forgotten port, with a small fishing community and pleasant beach with both pipeline and beginner waves for all levels of surfers.

PUNTA HERMOSA

A half hour south of Lima at Km 40 of the Panamericana, Punta Hermosa is a big-time surfing destination with a great range of beaches and services. It is here that **Pico Alto,**

© RENÉE DEL GAUDIO AND ROSS WEHNER

Lima's coastline is known as the Costa Verde because of the green vegetation that clings to portions of the ocean bluffs.

the largest wave in South America, forms in May and reaches heights of up to 12 meters. The town itself is on a rocky peninsula, called La Isla, which is surrounded by seven beaches. From north to south, these are El Silencio, Caballeros, Señoritas, Pico Alto, Playa Norte, La Isla, and Kontiki. When covered in rocks and not sand June–November, Playa Norte is a good place to get away from crowds, along with Kontiki. But wherever you stay in Punta Hermosa, these beaches are no more than a half-hour walk away.

Entertainment and Events

Every May or June, during the first big swell of the year, Punta Hermosa comes alive with Peru's annual big-wave competition. There is no fixed date for the competition and it is usually organized within a week or two—check out www.buoyweather.com (you have to pay) or www.stormsurf.com (free) for the right ocean conditions, or stayed tuned to www.peruazul.com, the country's premier **surfing** website.

Otherwise nightlife is clustered around the entry to Punta Hermosa and the few pubs on the waterfront.

Recreation

Punta Hermosa has several places to rent a board and wetsuit, get an instructor, and **surf** a variety of waves from gentle to suicidal. The best beginner beaches in Punta Hermosa are Caballeros, Pacharacas, and La Isla. Taxis and surfing camps can arrange transportation to beginner beaches farther south, such as Puerto Viejo and Cerro Azul.

The honest and straightforward **Marco León Villarán** (tel. 01/230-8316 or 01/230-8351, www.peruadventure.com), who runs a bed-and-breakfast in town, can arrange a variety of fabulous adventures in the area. His main passion is **spear fishing,** and if you have the snorkel, fins, and mask he can lead you to just about any fish you have ever dreamed of seeing—or spearing—including 1.2-meter yellowtail or gigantic flounder near Punta Hermosa. In his Zodiac with outboard motor, he also leads trips to nearby Isla Pachacamac (US$25 pp) for the rare opportunity to see Humboldt penguins, sea lions, and the occasional sea otter (known in Spanish as *gato de mar* because of its catlike appearance).

Marco is also a professional bone-and-fossil hunter who knows Peru's desert coastline very well—from the fossil-rich deserts of Ica to the pristine and remote surfing beaches north of Chiclayo. He owns a reliable four-wheel-drive van and is an excellent, affordable, and trustworthy option for getting into remote areas of the Ica desert. Like all fossil hunters, Marco keeps in touch with all the local *huaqeros*, or grave robbers, and can even arrange an opportunity to witness their ceremonies. Before they begin digging at midnight, they read coca leaves and drink *aguardiente* to protect themselves from evil spirits. He charges a US$50 daily guiding fee and then bills travelers for gas, food, and other expenses, probably another US$50 per day for a group of up to four people. He speaks Spanish only.

Accommodations

Punta Hermosa's better places are in La Planicie, a quiet neighborhood to the north of town that offers a nice respite from the rowdy surfer scene in town, a 10-minute walk away. A good restaurant and Internet access are nearby, along with Señoritas and Caballeros beaches. There are more hotels and nightlife, and the monster Pico Alto wave itself, near the center of Punta Hermosa—along with crowds of rowdy Brazilian and Argentinean surfers who are in town to test their mettle on waves that have made Punta Hermosa known as the Hawaii of South America. Nearly all of the hotels below offer full pension—for another US$10–15 per day, you can take all your meals at your hostel. This is an excellent deal and a good way to avoid stomach issues.

Finding a room for under US$15 a night is possible but not easy in Punta Hermosa's high season. The best bet is to simply walk around town and look for signs that say Se Alquilan Cuartos (Rooms Are Rented Here)—these can often be clean and as cheap as US$8 pp per night. Surfer hostels spring up in Punta Hermosa in the summer and are listed at www.peruazul. com. We found many of these to be noisy, so choose carefully. For a mere US$12, Cebichería Carmencita will set up a tent on the beach for up to seven people and make a campfire.

In the Planicie neighborhood, long-time Punta Hermosa resident Marco León Villarán offers something for everyone at the **Peru Adventure Lodge** (Block Ñ, Lote 1, La Planicie, tel. 01/230-8316 or 01/230-8351, www.peruadventure.com, US$20 pp). His rooms are quiet, large, and comfortable, with tons of hot water and two labrador retrievers who can lick you awake every morning for a bit extra. He and his wife, Gloria, prepare excellent meals and his sons, Daniel and Joaquín, are excellent, English-speaking surfing instructors (US$10 for two hours). The family rents out boards and also organizes surf and fossil tours all along the Peruvian coast.

A good friend of Marco's, right around the corner, is Flavio Solaria, a surfboard shaper and international surfing judge who runs **Señoritas Surf Camp** (Block Ñ, Lote 4, tel. 01/230-7578, srtsurfcamp@yahoo.com, US$20 pp, full board). "What I offer is a lifestyle," explains Flavio. "A surfer's pension." The wooden rooms are smaller and simpler than Marco's, with tapestries from Bali and nice lighting. Rooms range from simple bunks to a private room with queen-size beds. Flavio also sells his extraordinary boards (US$300 for short, US$620 for long) and rents both boards (US$10/day) and wetsuits (US$5/day). He happily takes guests to nearby beaches and teaches them to surf at no additional charge.

A final surf camp in Planicie is the **Punta Hermosa Surf Camp** (Block R, Lote 19, tel. 01/230-8357, puntasurfcamp@hotmail.com).

In Punta Hermosa, **Hostal La Isla** (Malecón Central 943, tel. 01/230-7146, sandrolaisla@ hotmail.com, US$16 s, US$30 d) is a relaxed guesthouse run by the family of longtime Punta Hermosa resident and surfer Sandro Testino. Though a bit more expensive than the rest, Hostal La Isla is on Punta Hermosa's beach promenade, has nice ocean views, and is close to town but still quiet at night. The rooms are simple but comfortable with nice shared terraces. Services include laundry, surfboard rental, transport to surfing areas, and Internet. Another camp is run by Oscar Morante, a surf guide who leads trips all around Peru for several international surfing agencies. His **Pico**

Alto International Surf Camp (Block L, Lote 14, tel. 01/230-7297, www.picoalto.com.pe, US$25–35 pp, full board) is well worth it.

A final good hostel, also near the center, is **Hospedaje Nylamp Wasi** (Pacasmayo 167, tel. 01/230-8401, surfperu50@hotmail.com, US$10 s, US$20 d, including breakfast).

Hotel La Rotonda (Bolognesi 580, above the restaurant of the same name, tel. 01/230-7390, larotondasurfcamp@hotmail.com, US$20 s, US$40 d) has eight nice rooms with ocean views and cable TV. These are right near the bars, however, and probably get noisy at night.

One of the nicest places to stay on the Peruvian coast, and one of the better values, must be **Casa Barco** (Punta Hermosa 340, tel. 01/230-7081, www.casabarco.com, US$18 dorm, US$55–72 d with breakfast). A five-minute walk from the center, this small and friendly hostel has a great pool with whirlpool tub, a beautiful flower garden, and a classy bar/restaurant with a full, reasonably priced menu of ceviche and other fish dishes. The rooms have black-and-white floor tiles, luxurious beds, cable TV, wraparound porches with ocean views, and huge, beautiful showers. Shared rooms are much simpler, but clean with access to all the hotel's services. The best part, however, is the art. The owners, ceramic artist Teresa Carvallo and writer Felix Portocarrera, have assembled a mind-blowing collection of contemporary art from Peru's best painters and sculptors.

Food

There are many seafood restaurants, but probably the safest is **La Rotonda** (Bolognesi 592, tel. 01/230-7266, 8 A.M.–11 P.M. daily, US$5). Apart from ceviche, the restaurant also does *chicharron* and grilled fish, serving on a second-story deck with good views of surfers on Pico Alto. Another option is **Cebichería Carmencita** (Malecón de Punta Hermosa 821, tel. 01/9976-4792, 7 A.M.–10 P.M. daily, US$5), which serves a range of fish dishes; the owner will even set up a tent and campfire for you. At Señoritas beach, ask around for the ceviche stall run by Paco and Cecilia, which has a good reputation among locals.

For Italian check out **Donde Luis** on the Punta Hermosa waterfront or, in La Planicie, **Trattoria Don Ángelo** (near control gate, tel. 01/230-7104 or 01/9740-9982, 7 A.M.–midnight daily, US$5). This is a family-run store and restaurant that serves pizzas and homemade pastas, including lasagna, ravioli, cannelloni, and gnocchi.

Getting There and Around

Probably the easiest way to get to Punta Hermosa from Lima is to hire a taxi (US$10) or arrange a pickup through your hotel. **Flavio Solaria** (tel. 01/230-7578, srtsurfcamp@yahoo.com) picks up groups from the Lima airport for US$25. Buses for Mala—which stop outside of Punta Hermosa, San Bartolo, and Santa María—pick up passengers at the circle, or *trébol,* where Avenida Javier Prado intersects the Panamericana in Monterrico. These buses, called Maleños, take 45 minutes to reach Punta Hermosa and charge US$0.75.

Three-wheeled *motocars* abound in Punta Hermosa and are a US$0.50 option for getting between La Planicie and the town center.

SAN BARTOLO

Farther down the Panamericana, past an exclusive area of homes perched on a seaside cliff and an exclusive beach club known as La Quebrada, lies the laid-back beach town of San Bartolo. The town itself is perched on a bluff above an attractive horseshoe-shaped beach, lined with hotels, condos, and a *malecón,* known as Playa Norte. San Bartolo is less of a surfer party spot than the center of Punta Hermosa, even with Peñascal, a right reef break that gets as high as four meters on the south end of the Playa Norte. There are gentler waves and a good place for swimming on the north end of Playa Norte, along with a few nice beachfront hotels. After entering from Km 48 of the Panamericana, the main drag into town is Avenida San Bartolo. Most hotels are along Mar Pacífico, a street that runs to the left (south). To the right, another road leads around to Kahunas Hostal and Playa Norte.

Entertainment and Events

San Bartolo's best disco, **Peñascal**, is near the town's highway entrance and is only open during the summer.

Accommodations

Prices in San Bartolo double on weekend nights, so if you are planning a budget trip, make sure to visit during weekdays. Prices listed are for weekdays.

On the bluff above town, **Playa Mar Hostal** (San Bartolo 211, tel. 01/430-7247, US$18 s or d) is a surfer's hangout with brick walls, bamboo ceilings, tile floors, and private bathrooms. Another good option, and much cleaner than a few other hostels nearby, is **Hostal La Marina** (San Martín 351, tel. 01/430-7601, US$15 s or d). About half the 20 rooms have ocean views; it also offers cable TV, restaurant, and all-you-can-drink potable water.

For what it is, **Hostal 800** (Malecón 800, tel. 01/430-7514, US$25 d, cheaper by the week) is a great value. This hotel, like the others on the beach, is built up onto the hillside, so all the rooms have great ocean views. But these apartments are huge and luxurious, each with a private porch and commodious bedroom. An extra US$5 buys you a separate kitchen with fridge and microwave. There are also slightly cheaper rooms without terraces for US$15 a night. The owners of Hostal 800 also have **Hostal 110** (Malecón 110, tel. 01/430-7559, US$30 d, cheaper by the week) on the south end of the beach, a similar setup with even larger two-bedroom apartments.

Great service and plush surroundings can be found at **Sol y Mar** (Malecón 930, tel. 01/892-1999, US$27 s, US$42 d), with white leather couches, huge tiled rooms, great bathrooms, cable TV, fridges, full kitchens in a few rooms, and terraces with great ocean-view rooms. The other nice place on Playa Norte is **La Posada del Mirador** (Malecón 105, tel. 01/430-7822, www.posadadelmirador.com, US$20 s, US$25 d with breakfast), with furnished apartments.

Peruvian surfing champion Makki Block rents surfboards and offers lessons from his **Kahunas Hostal** (tel. 01/430-7407, US$20 s, US$35 d

with breakfast). The hostel is perched on a bluff at the north end of Playa Norte and overlooks the Peñascal surfing break. Perks include a secluded terrace, pool, hydromassage, and TVs in all the rooms, which are decorated with surf decor.

Food

Most of the eating options—except for the spit-roasted chicken at Mar Pacífico 495—revolve around seafood. **Restaurant Curazao** (San Bartolo 231, tel. 01/430-7787, 8 A.M.–5 P.M. daily, US$3–5) is known for its Peruvian seafood plates, but can also make Chilean dishes upon request. There's a line of restaurants down Mar Pacífico. The best of these include **El Arador del Mar** (Mar Pacífico, tel. 01/430-8215, US$3–5), with a good seafood lunch menu for US$3. But the next-door **El Rincón de Chelulo** (Mar Pacífico s/n, tel. 01/430-7170) wins out for a greater variety of fish and shellfish, unbelievable friendly service, and a larger US$3 lunch menu. These restaurants are in front of the plaza where the town's market opens up every morning. This square also holds a few ice cream shops and pizzerias, open in summer only.

Information and Services

The best place for local info is the town's chamber of commerce, which can respond to questions in Spanish via email at **sanbartoloperu@ yahoo.es**. Or check the surfers' website **www. peruazul.com**. Both the **police** and the **local clinic** are on Avenida San Bartolo near the highway entrance. There is Internet at **Mar Pacífico 495** (tel. 01/430-7137, US$0.60 per hour), which is also a surf shop.

Getting There and Around

Probably the easiest way to get to San Bartolo from Lima is to hire a taxi (US$15) or take the Cruz del Sur bus, which stops at the town entrance. Local buses for Mala—which stop outside of Punta Hermosa, San Bartolo, and Santa María—pick up passengers at the circle, or *trébol,* where Avenida Javier Prado intersects with the Panamericana in Barranco. These buses, called Maleños, take 50 minutes to reach San Bartolo and charge US$0.75.

www.moon.com

DESTINATIONS | ACTIVITIES | BLOGS | MAPS | BOOKS

MOON.COM is ready to help plan your next trip! Filled with fresh trip ideas and strategies, author interviews, informative travel blogs, a detailed map library, and descriptions of all the Moon guidebooks, Moon.com is all you need to get out and explore the world—or even places in your own backyard. While at Moon.com, sign up for our monthly e-newsletter for updates on new releases, travel tips, and expert advice from our on-the-go Moon authors. As always, when you travel with Moon, expect an experience that is uncommon and truly unique.

MOON IS ON FACEBOOK—BECOME A FAN!
JOIN THE MOON PHOTO GROUP ON FLICKR

MAP SYMBOLS

▬▬▬	Expressway	【	Highlight	✖	Airfield	♁	Golf Course
·········	Primary Road	○	City/Town	✖	Airport	P	Parking Area
═══════	Secondary Road	◉	State Capital	▲	Mountain	▰	Archaeological Site
░░░░░░	Unpaved Road	⊛	National Capital	✛	Unique Natural Feature	⚲	Church
- - - - -	Trail	★	Point of Interest			⛽	Gas Station
··············	Ferry	●	Accommodation	🕊	Waterfall	⬭	Glacier
▪▪▪▪▪	Railroad	▼	Restaurant/Bar	▲	Park		Mangrove
▓▓▓▓▓	Pedestrian Walkway	■	Other Location	🚩	Trailhead		Reef
▥▥▥▥	Stairs	⋀	Campground	⛷	Skiing Area		Swamp

CONVERSION TABLES

°C = (°F - 32) / 1.8
°F = (°C x 1.8) + 32
1 inch = 2.54 centimeters (cm)
1 foot = 0.304 meters (m)
1 yard = 0.914 meters
1 mile = 1.6093 kilometers (km)
1 km = 0.6214 miles
1 fathom = 1.8288 m
1 chain = 20.1168 m
1 furlong = 201.168 m
1 acre = 0.4047 hectares
1 sq km = 100 hectares
1 sq mile = 2.59 square km
1 ounce = 28.35 grams
1 pound = 0.4536 kilograms
1 short ton = 0.90718 metric ton
1 short ton = 2,000 pounds
1 long ton = 1.016 metric tons
1 long ton = 2,240 pounds
1 metric ton = 1,000 kilograms
1 quart = 0.94635 liters
1 US gallon = 3.7854 liters
1 Imperial gallon = 4.5459 liters
1 nautical mile = 1.852 km

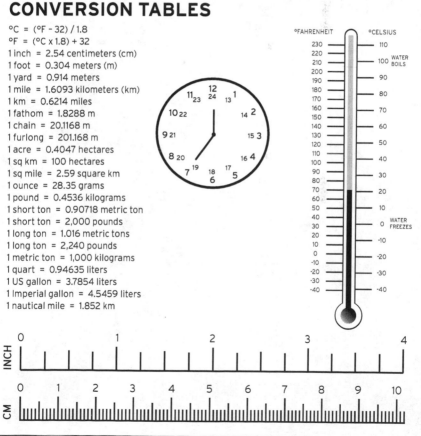

MOON SPOTLIGHT LIMA

Avalon Travel
a member of the Perseus Books Group
1700 Fourth Street
Berkeley, CA 94710, USA
www.moon.com

Editor: Erin Raber
Series Manager: Kathryn Ettinger
Copy Editor: Deana Shields
Graphics and Production Coordinator: Darren Alessi
Map Editor: Albert Angulo
Cartographers: Kat Bennett, Mike Morgenfeld,
 Chris L. Henrick, Allison Rawley
Proofreader: Jamie Andrade

ISBN-13: 978-1-59880-672-4

Text © 2011 by Ross Wehner and Renée del Gaudio.
Maps © 2011 by Avalon Travel.
All rights reserved.

Some photos and illustrations are used by permission
and are the property of the original copyright owners.

Front cover photo: Monasterio de San Francisco, Lima,
 Peru © istockphoto.com
Title page photo: © Robert Lerich/123RF.com

ABOUT THE AUTHOR

Ross Wehner & Renée del Gaudio

Happiness, as Ross Wehner and Renée del Gaudio discovered, is an open road, a borrowed jeep, and an entire country to explore. They spent ten months – and eight flat tires – zigzagging across the Andes to find the best travel experiences Peru has to offer.

A highlight of Ross and Renée's research was kayaking across Lake Titicaca at dawn, with the orange orb of the sun popping over sapphire waters and lighting up a backdrop of snow-covered mountains. They climbed in the Cordillera Blanca, built a balsa raft in the Manu jungle, hiked the Inka Trail, and searched for lost cities in the Chachapoyas cloud forest.

Ross is founder of World Leadership School, an organization that helps young people learn to lead on global issues. Before that, he worked for seven years as a journalist in Peru and other Latin American countries. He has written for the *San Francisco Chronicle*, *Mother Jones*, *Ski*, and other publications, and has also worked as a wilderness educator for the National Outdoor Leadership School (NOLS). Ross holds a master's degree in Spanish and Latin American literature from the University of Virginia.

As an architect, Renée has long considered Machu Picchu to be the world's finest example of architecture integrating with the landscape. She runs her own architecture practice, Renée del Gaudio Architecture, focused on sustainable, modern design. Her designs have been published in *Dwell* and *House Beautiful*, which ranked her as one of the Top 25 Next Wave Designers in America. She holds a bachelor's degree from the University of Michigan and a master's degree in architecture from the University of Washington in Seattle.

Renée and Ross live in Denver, Colorado and have two children, Sebastian and Francesca.